AF473881

ANIMALS
IN WARTIME

Published by IWM, Lambeth Road, London SE1 6HZ
iwm.org.uk

ISBN 978-1-912423-44-6

A catalogue record for this book is available from the British Library.
Printed and bound by Gomer Press Limited
Colour reproduction by DL Imaging

Front cover: Venus, the Bulldog mascot of the destroyer HMS *Vansittart*, 1940.

Back cover: Swabby the puppy accompanies his owner, Chief Machinist's Mate Edward Hutton, in an invasion craft for the Allied landings in Normandy, France, on 6 June 1944.

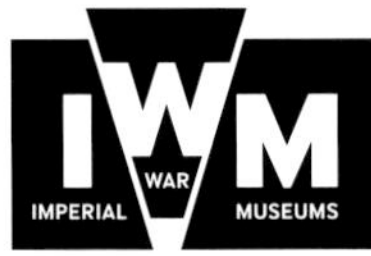

ANIMALS IN WARTIME

Simon Offord

INTRODUCTION

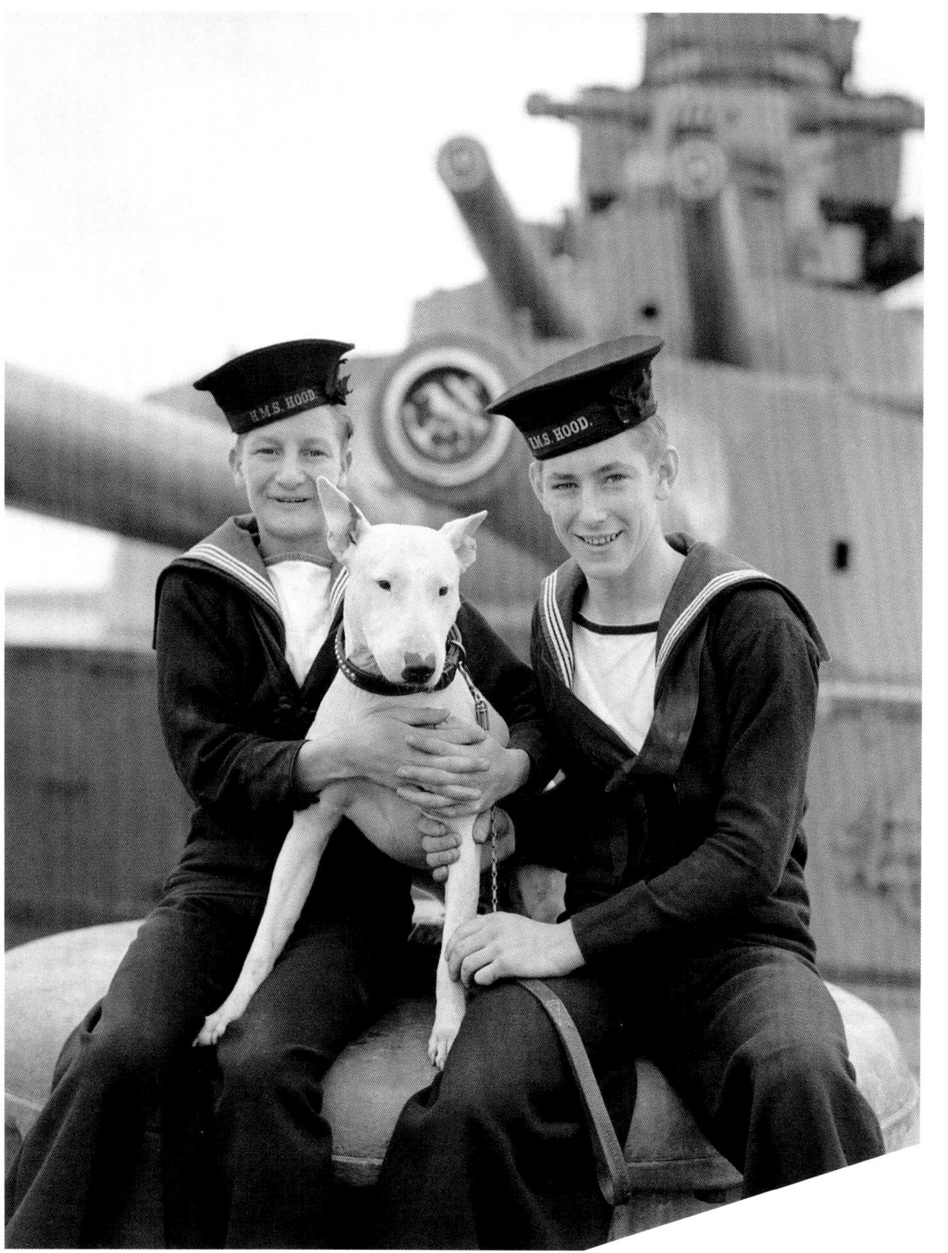

Two members of the crew of HMS *Hood* with unofficial mascot Bill, a Bull Terrier, 1940.

IWM holds 11 million photographs covering the causes, course and consequences of conflict from the First World War to present day. These photographs come from official, press and private sources, and cover all aspects of warfare. Some of the most popular photographs in the collection are those that show animals.

Animals have been used in warfare since the beginning of recorded history. However, from the start of the First World War armies grew to enormous sizes, and the numbers of animals needed to support them equally expanded. It is estimated that over 16 million animals served during the First World War alone.

At the height of the First World War, the Allies and Central Powers had a total of 103 cavalry divisions between them, totalling a million men. Millions of horses were used to carry these cavalrymen into battle, as well as to pull guns and waggons of supplies and other equipment into position. However, the static nature of trench warfare on the Western Front meant that cavalry units lost their usual mobility, and horses, donkeys and mules were therefore used primarily to transfer heavy loads across rough and varied terrain in this theatre. In the Middle East and Africa, camels and elephants were used alongside horses in a similar role. They were also usefully used to evacuate wounded people from areas where motor ambulances could not reach.

Animals were also vital for communication during the conflicts because, despite new radio technology, often the quickest and most reliable way to transport a message was by pigeon or dog. Indeed by the end of the First World War there were 22,000 pigeons in the British Army, and so valuable was this method of communication that killing or wounding a pigeon was an offence punishable by 6 months imprisonment or a £100 fine. Dogs also proved their worth: as well as physically carrying messages, they could be used to lay telephone cables quickly across battlefields.

With the coming of the Second World War, advances in communications and increasing mechanisation meant animals were not thought to be needed as much. By 1942 the British Army had only 6,500 horses, 10,000 mules and 1,700 camels in service. Despite this, almost 250,000 pigeons were used by Britain during the Second World War, many of which were acquired by the Royal Air Force (RAF) as a back up to radio equipment, and to accompany aircrews in case their aircraft crashed. Other new roles also emerged for animals during the Second World War. Dogs' abilities to sniff out hidden mines, and to locate wounded people either on the battlefield or in bombed out houses on the home front, made them invaluable.

While pigeons are no longer used by the military, and horses are now mostly used for ceremonial duties (with the last British pack units being disbanded in 1979), dogs are still the most versatile of animals used in active service by the military. Today they take on such diverse roles as guarding facilities, carrying messages, detecting landmines, explosives, and improvised explosive devices (IED's), locating casualties and tracking enemies.

During conflicts animals have also been subject to the same dangers faced by their owners. The Royal Society for the Prevention of Cruelty to Animals (RSPCA) has said that almost

Prevention of Cruelty to Animals (RSPCA) has said that almost half a million animals were killed by enemy action, disease or accident during the First World War, despite animal welfare being seen as paramount. Over 43,000 British soldiers worked in the Army Veterinary Corps (AVC) during the conflict, looking after two and a half million hospital admissions.

In the the Second World War, the re-named Royal Army Veterinary Corps (RAVC) had only 4,500 members as the need for this work decreased. Meanwhile, on the home front thousands of pets were euthanised at the beginning of the war due to fears of food shortages, and pets being injured or going feral after bombing. At the same time, the need for food to support the country was heightened, and farming became more intensive and organised. Thousands of women were called up to the Women's Land Army (WLA), often having to work with horses to till the land due to petrol rationing affecting tractors.

Soldiers who worked with animals appreciated their worth and cared for their welfare. However, animals were rarely given the official recognition they deserved. For instance, at the end of the First World War, thousands of horses were sold for meat rather than transported back to the UK. In 1943 Maria Dickin CBE, founder of the People's Dispensary for Sick Animals (PDSA) instituted the Dickin Medal, also known as the 'Animals' Victoria Cross'. It is awarded to animals serving with the Armed Forces or in Civil Defence units that have displayed outstanding acts of bravery or devotion. Between 1943 and 1949, and from 2000 to 2022 when the medal was revived, the Dickin Medal was awarded to thirty-two pigeons, thirty-seven dogs, five horses (including one honorary medal representing all horses and other animals killed during the First World War) and one ship's cat.

Yet it wasn't just for their abilities and usefulness that animals were kept around. They were used as mascots for different units. Some were in an official capacity, where they would be given a uniform and perform in ceremonial duties, but most would be unofficial – pets or strays that were adopted by service men and women. The morale boost was immense as these pets would provide comfort and distractions from conditions. Photographs of these mascots, taken by the Army Film and Photographic Units, and by the Ministry of Information (MOI), provided heart-warming stories that distracted people from the grim realities of war.

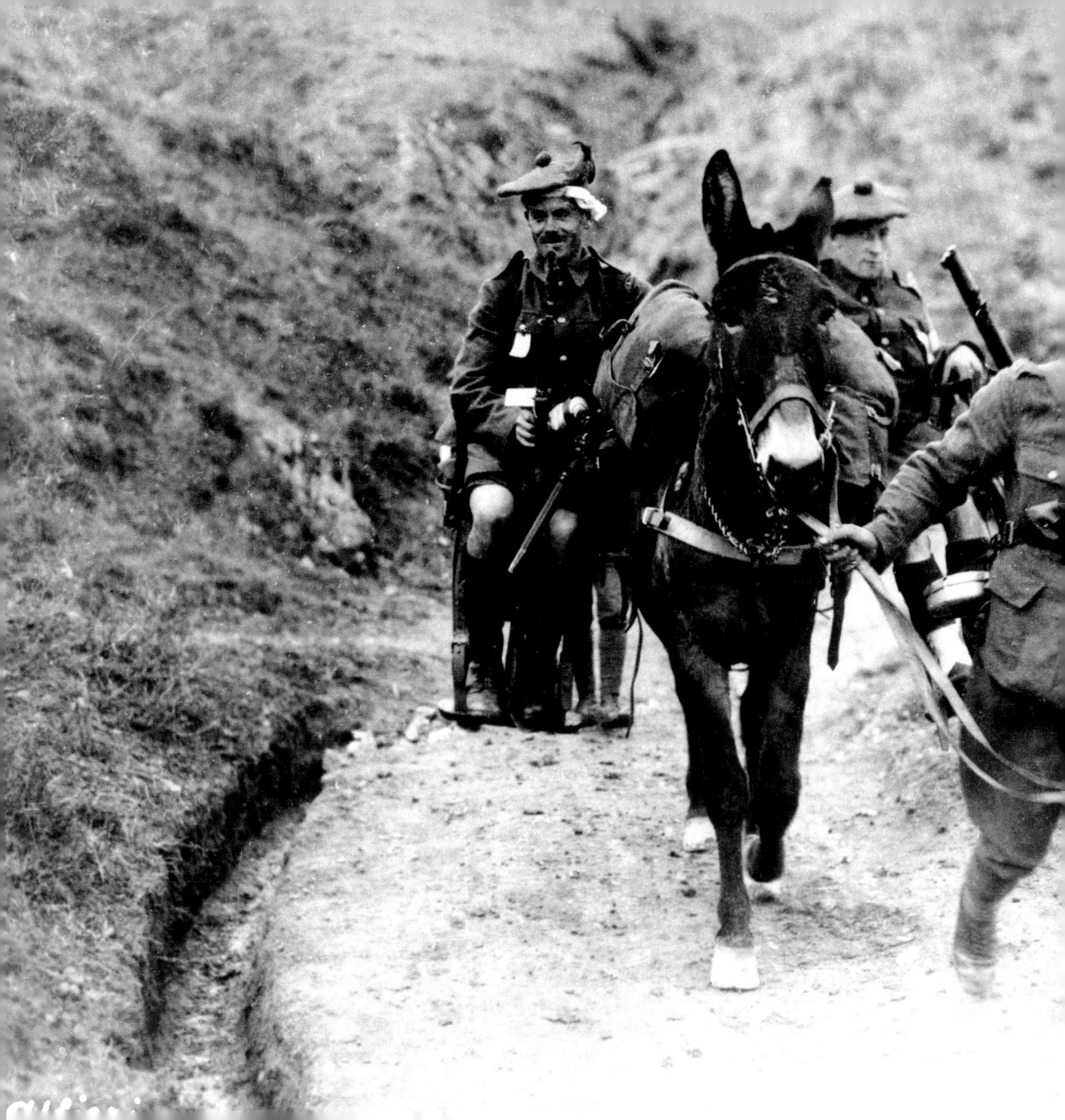

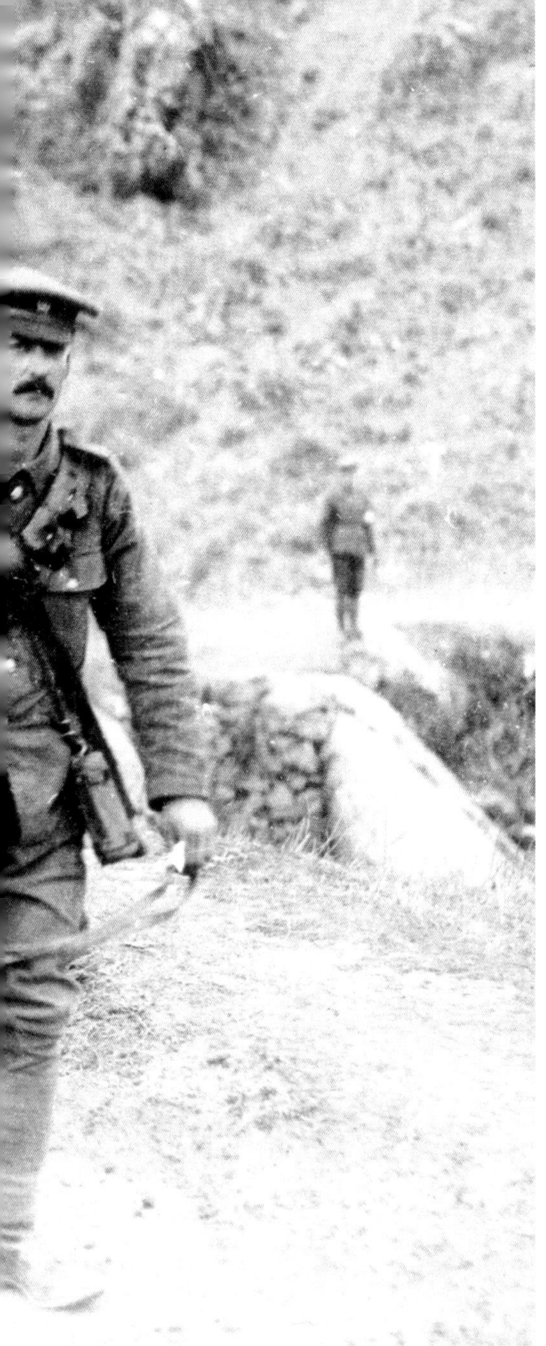

Casualties from 77th Brigade being brought to a dressing station by mule-borne cacolet (panniers designed to hold seats or stretchers for sick or wounded people) during the Salonika Campaign, February 1916.

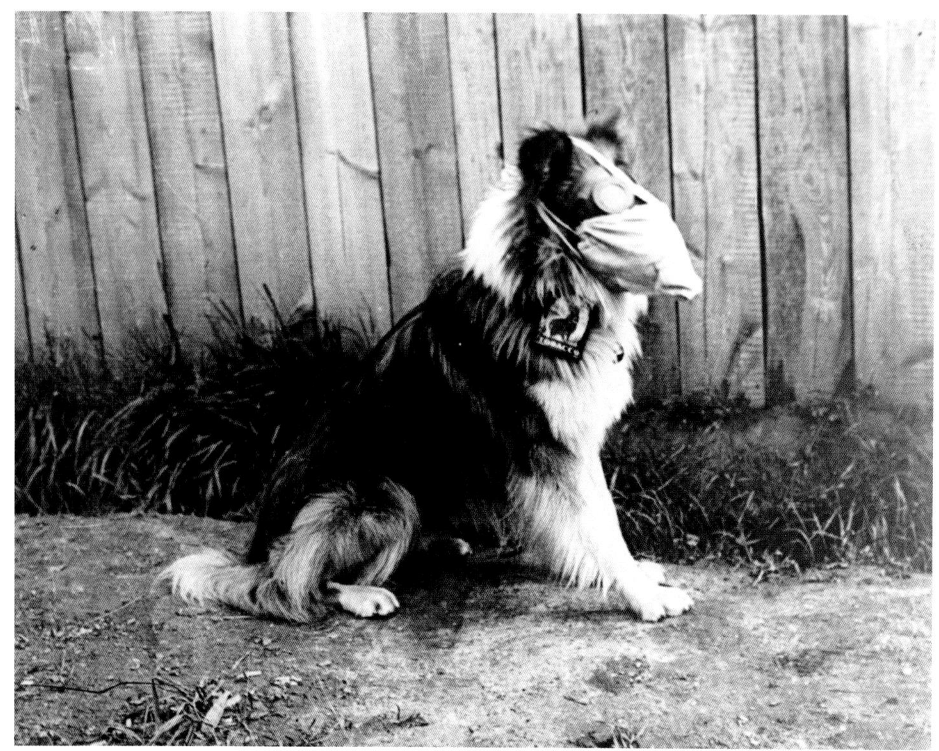

Horses and dogs were just as susceptible to gas attacks as humans, and measures were taken to protect them. This dog is wearing a gas mask and anti-gas goggles at the military kennels at Roesbrugge, Belgium, 16 May 1916.

British troops applying bandages to wounded horses, October 1916. Over 43,000 British soldiers served in the Army Veterinary Corps during the First World War, while in France alone the RSPCA treated over 720,000 sick and wounded animals.

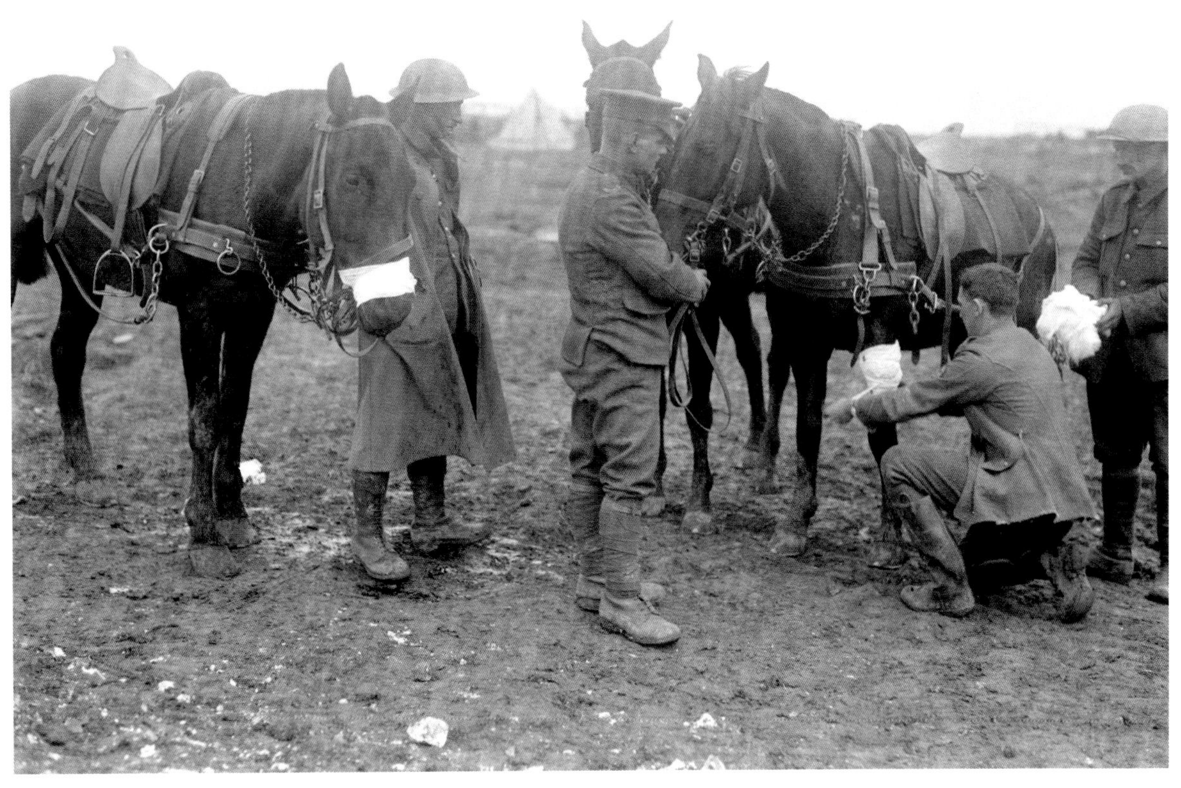

During heavy rains, mules and heavy vehicles of the Nigerian Brigade were taken across the Ruwu River by cable, in German East Africa, April 1917. Strong, but stubborn, mules were very versatile in rough terrain and could carry heavy loads.

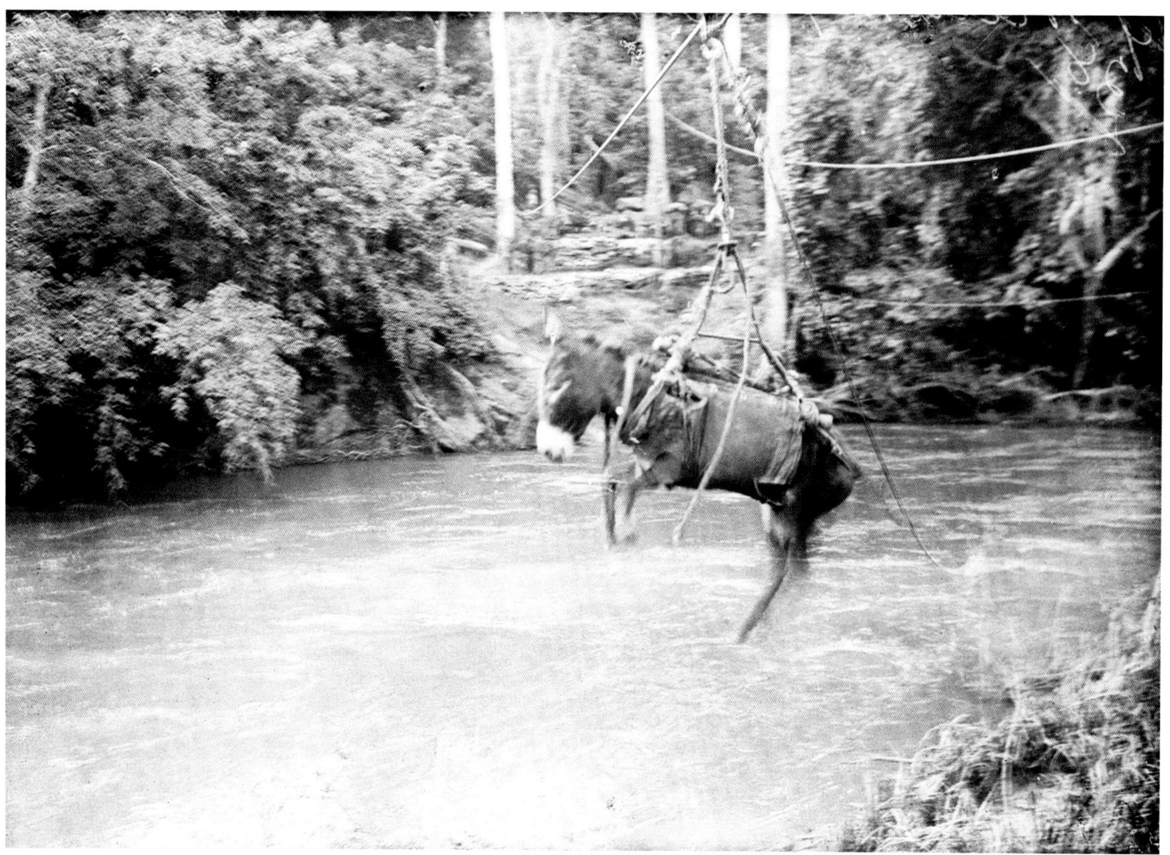

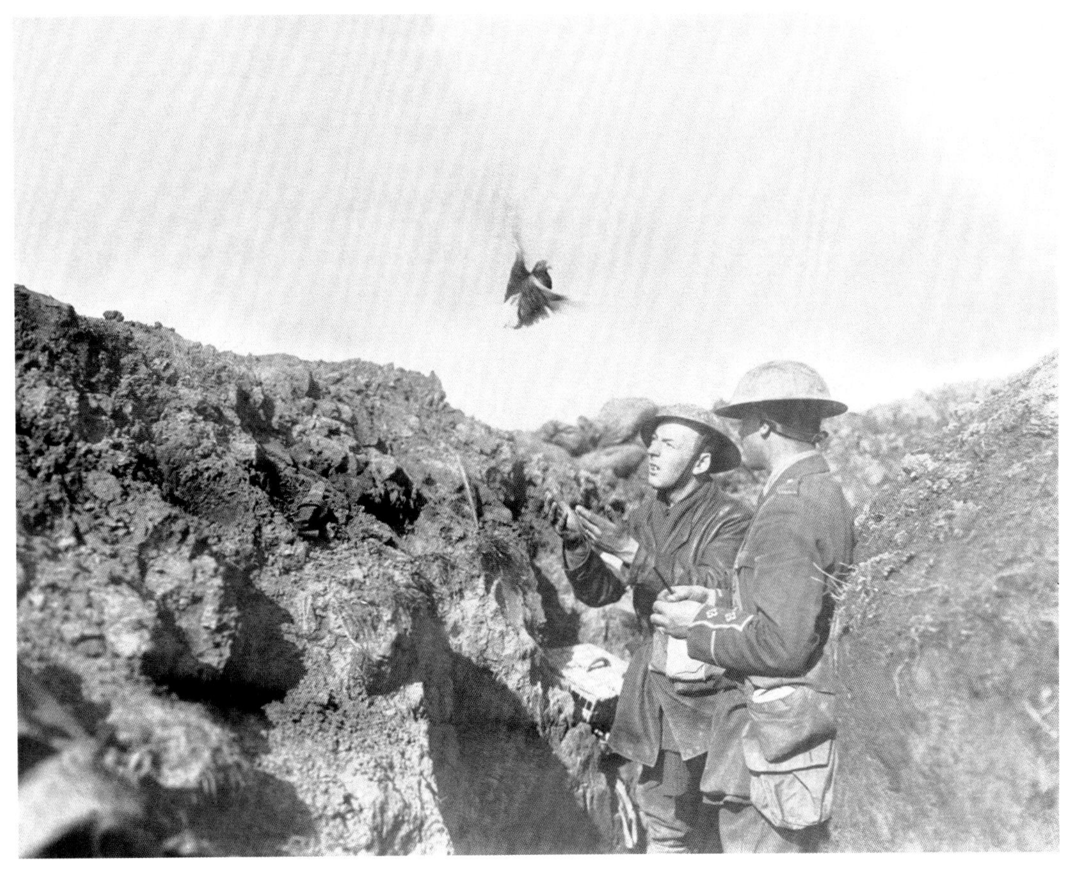

Canadian soldiers release a carrier pigeon from a trench on the Western Front, May 1917. By the end of the First World War, it is estimated that there were 22,000 pigeons in the British Army, looked after by 400 pigeoneers.

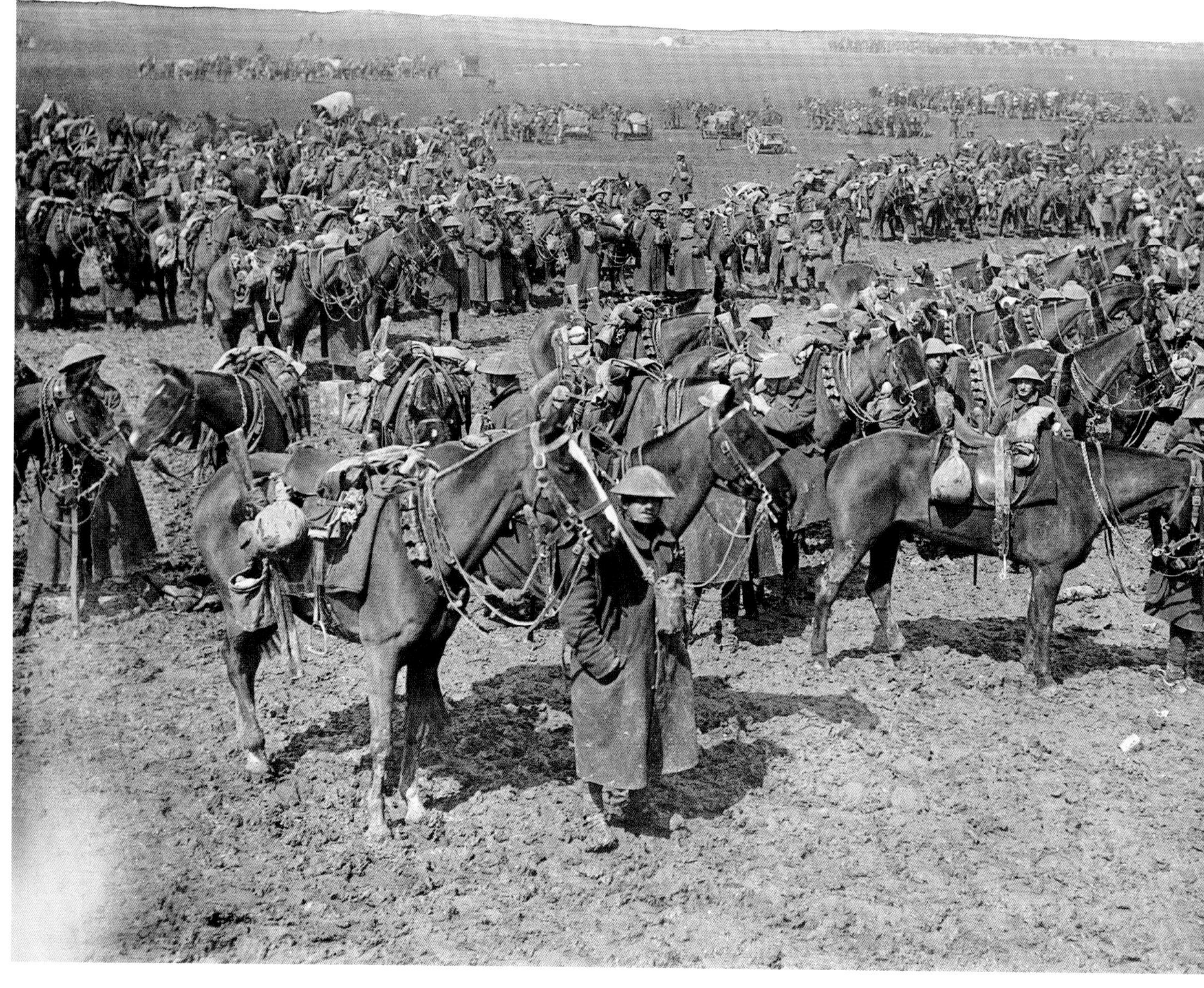

British cavalry wait for orders to move forward during operations in the Arras sector, 26 May 1917. At the start of the First World War the British Army had only 23,000 horses, but within weeks it had over 150,000.

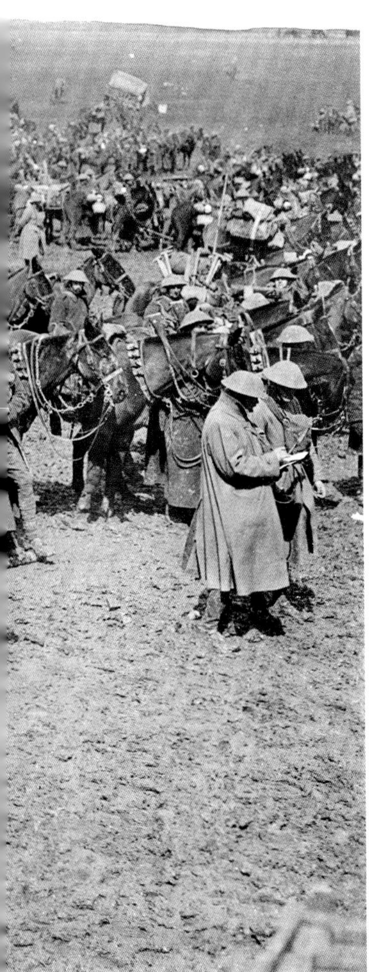

Dromedary camels fitted with cacolet panniers carry wounded men to safety on the North West Frontier of India, July 1917.

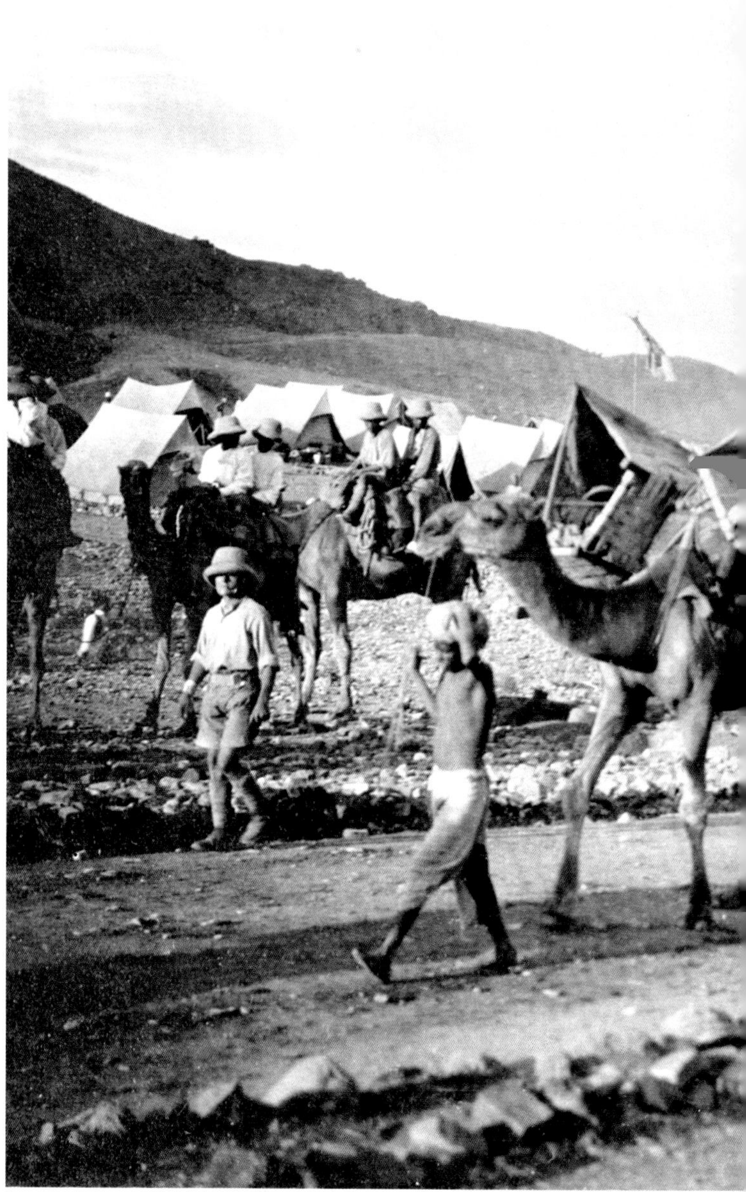

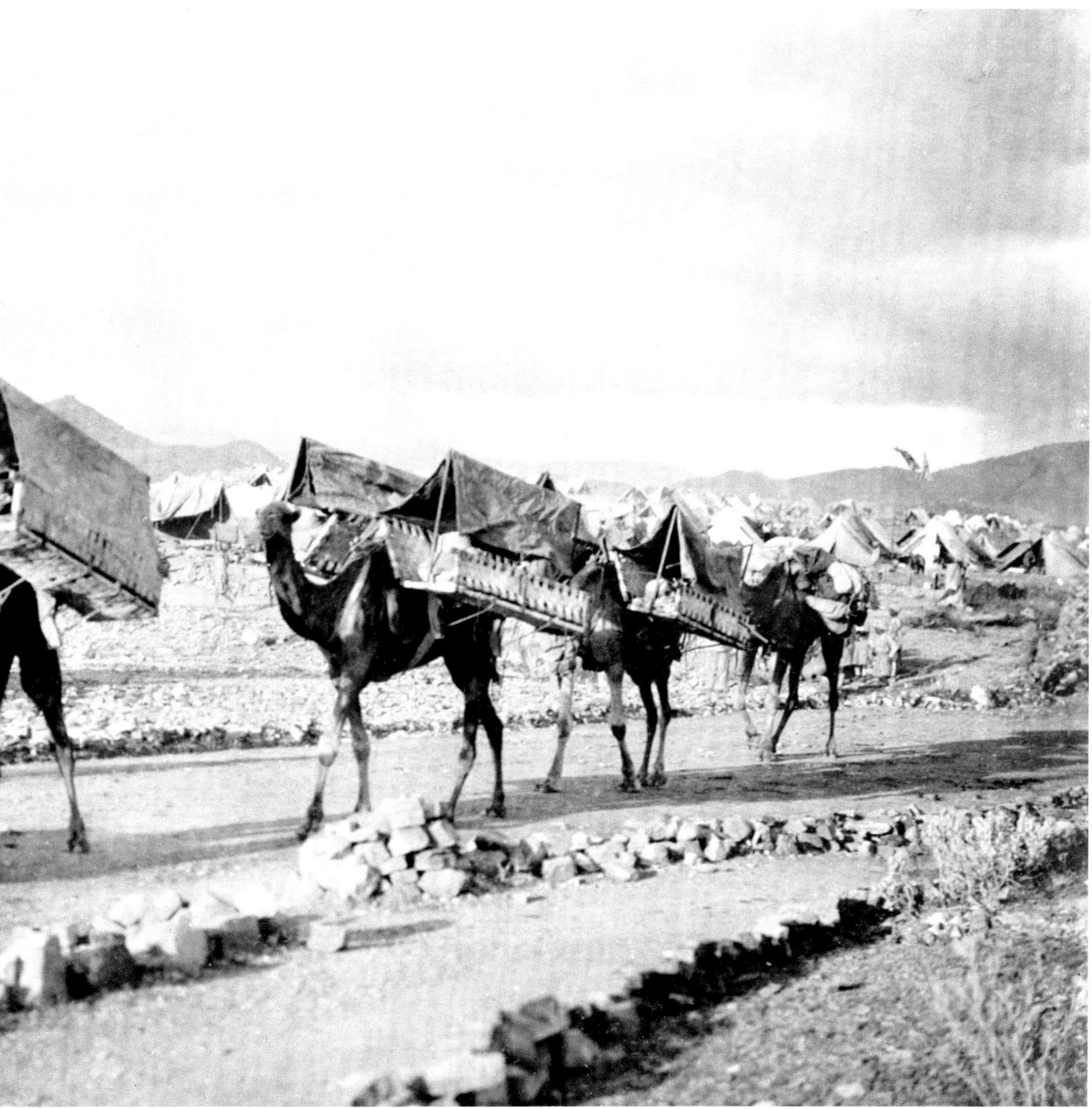

Queenie, a dog-mascot of the 3rd and 4th London Field Ambulances Royal Army Medical Corps, recovering a 'wounded' soldier during a training session at the Duke of York's Headquarters in Chelsea, London, 1917.

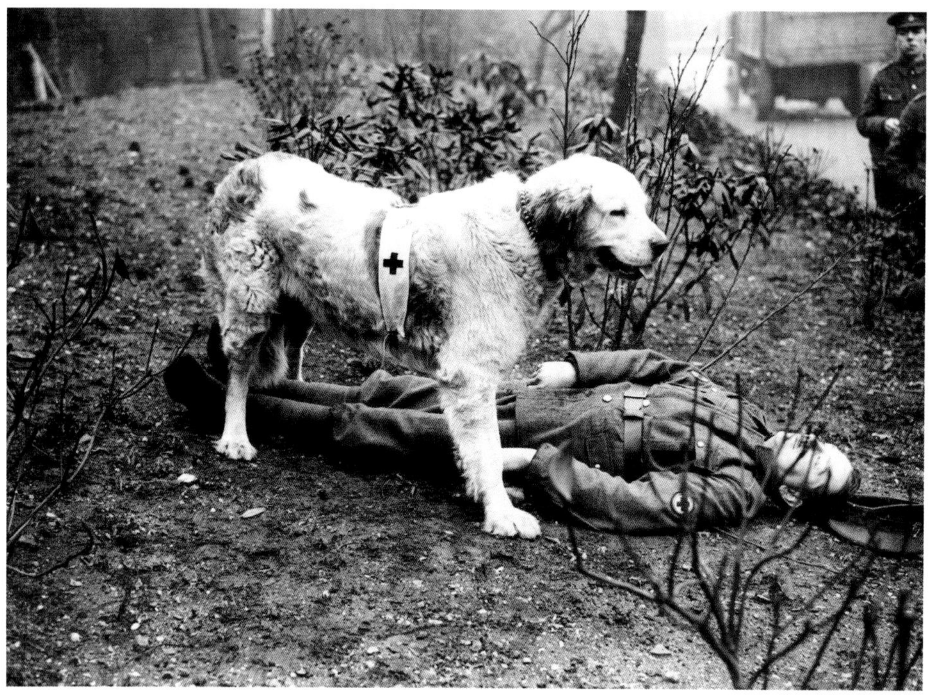

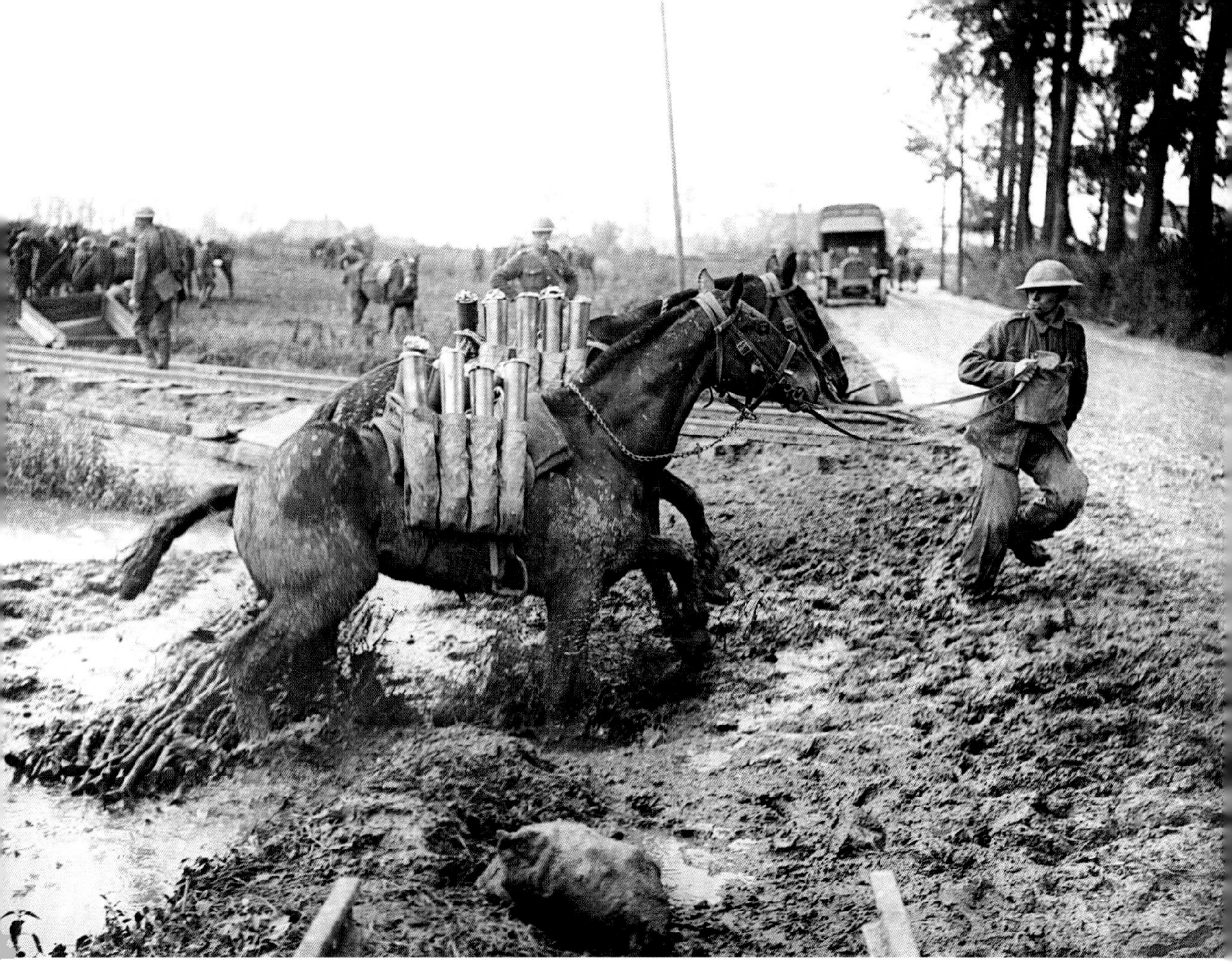

Two pack mules carrying shells in carriers struggle through the mud near Ypres, Belgium, during the battle of Pilckem Ridge, August 1917.

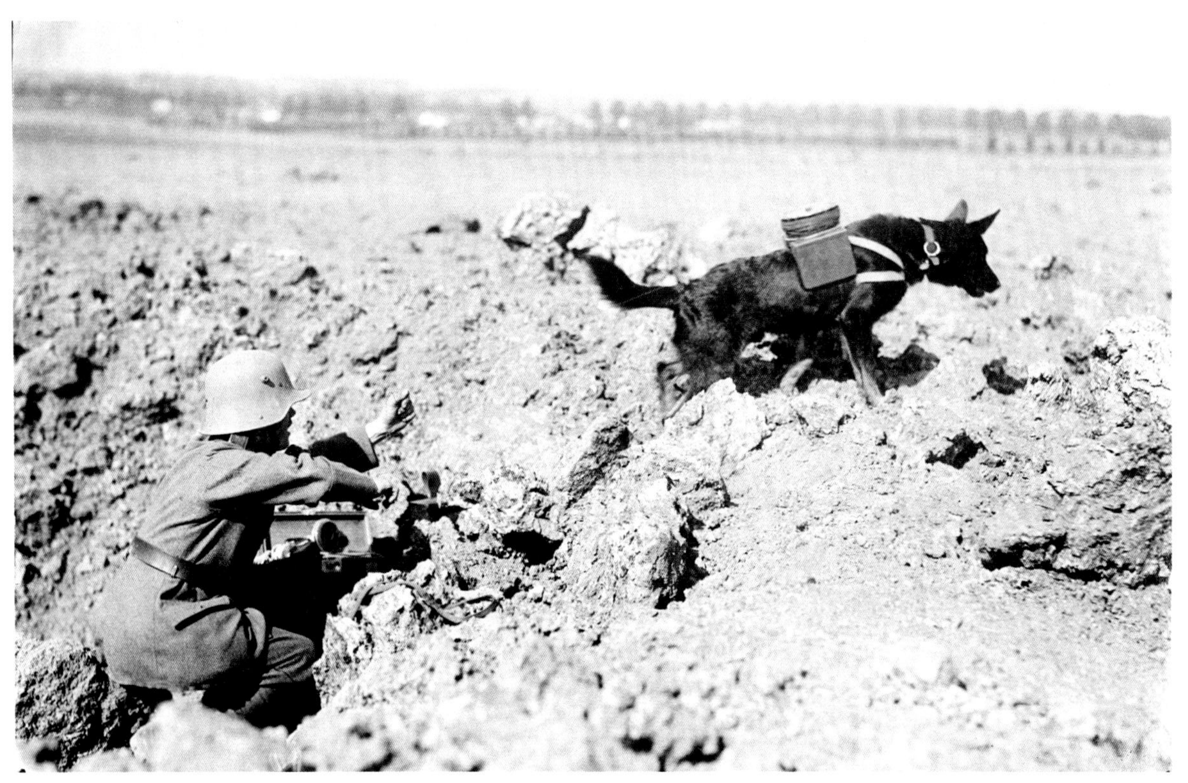

A German signaller releasing a dog carrying apparatus for laying telephone wires from a trench, Western Front, September 1917.

A trench message dog of the 5th Battalion, Manchester Regiment, waits for an officer to complete the note he is writing, Cuinchy, France, 26 January 1918. The dog's collar has a cylinder attached which would hold the message.

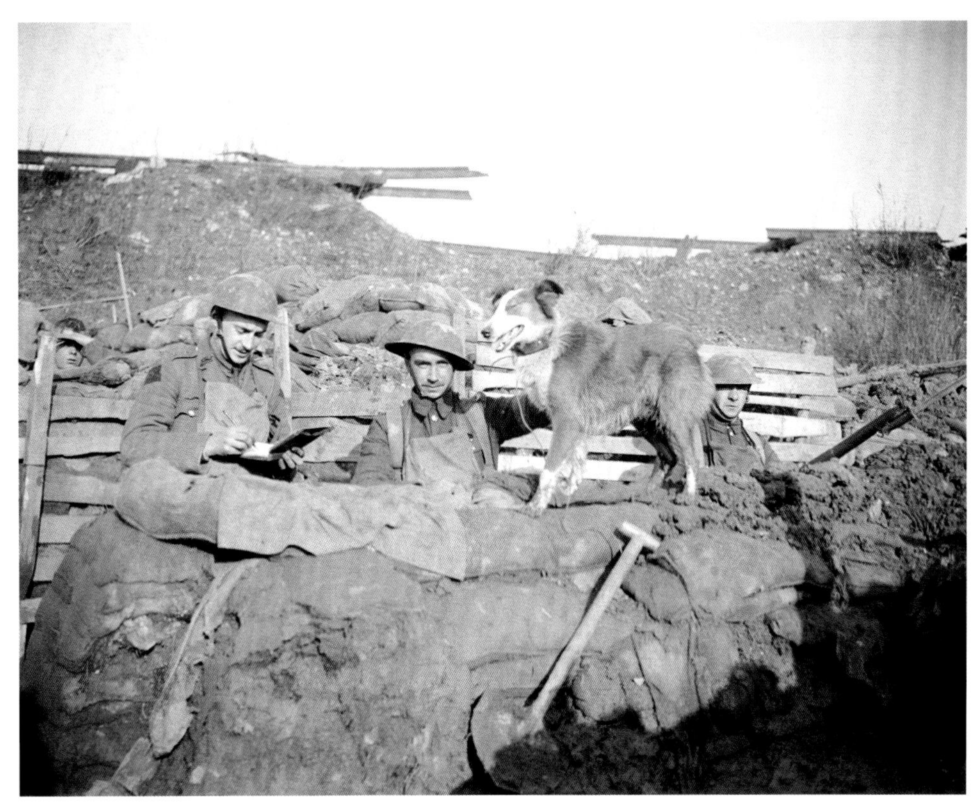

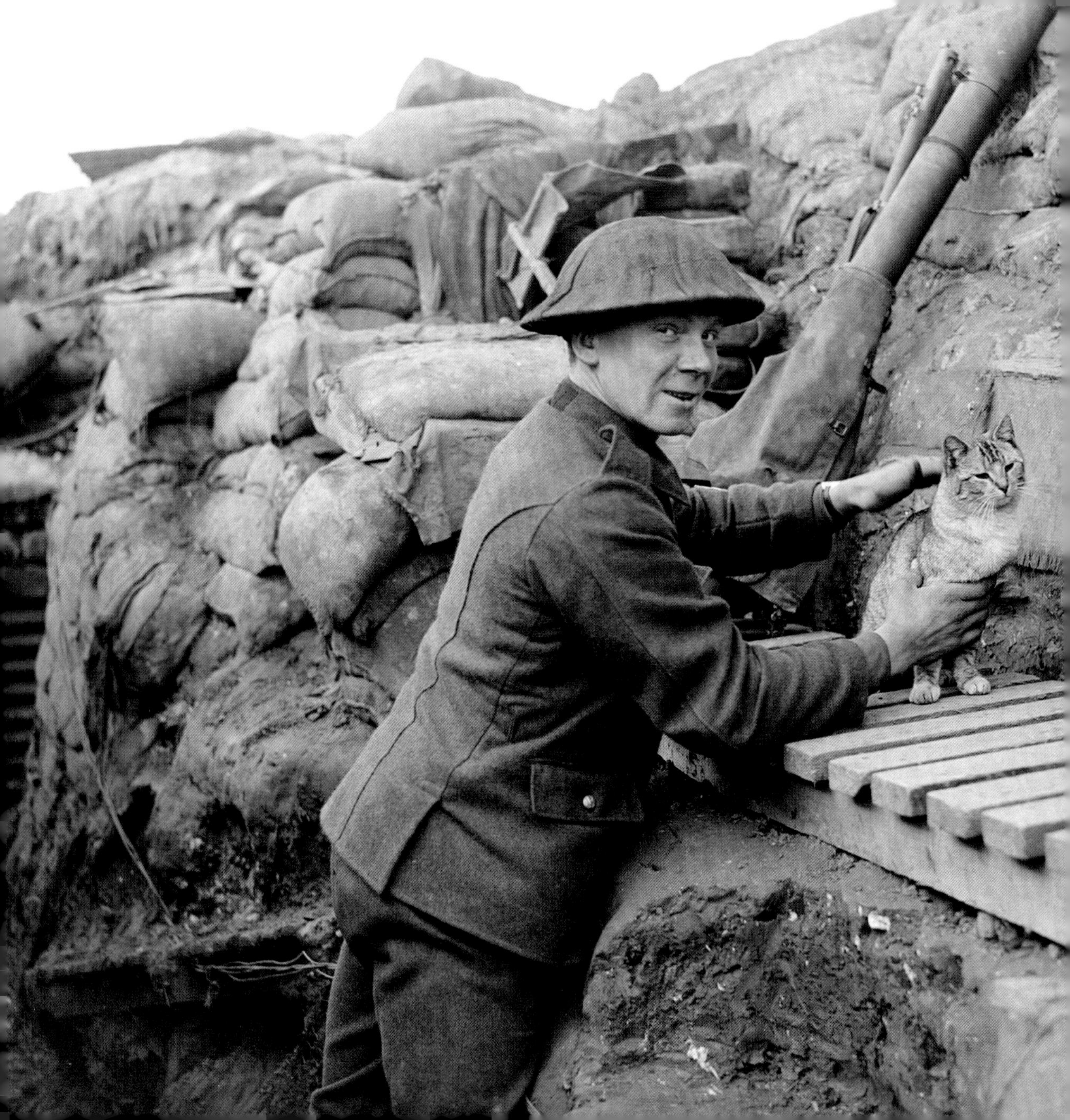

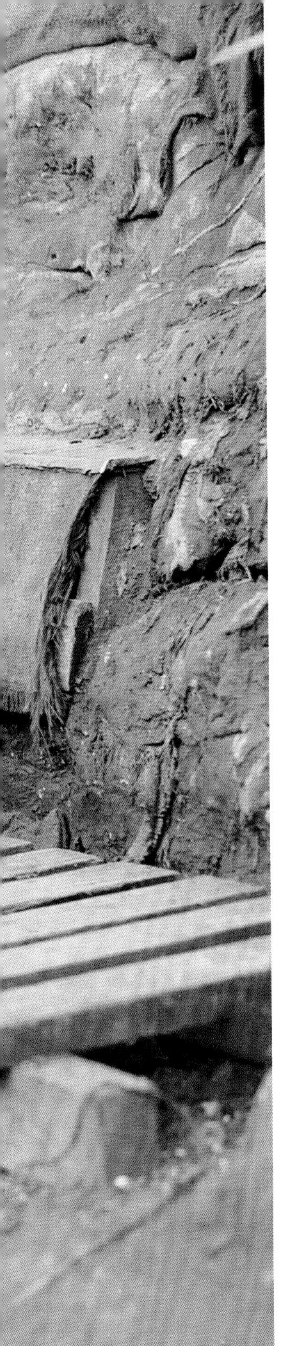

A Lewis gunner of the 6th Battalion, the York and Lancaster Regiment, with the Regiment's cat mascot, in a trench near Cambrin, France, 6 February 1918. As well helping against rats in the trenches, cats helped bring comfort to the soldiers.

Female trainers of the Army Remount Service (ARS) taking a horse and a mule over jumps at Underdale Hall, near Shrewsbury, 1918. A third of a million British horses passed through the ARS during the First World War.

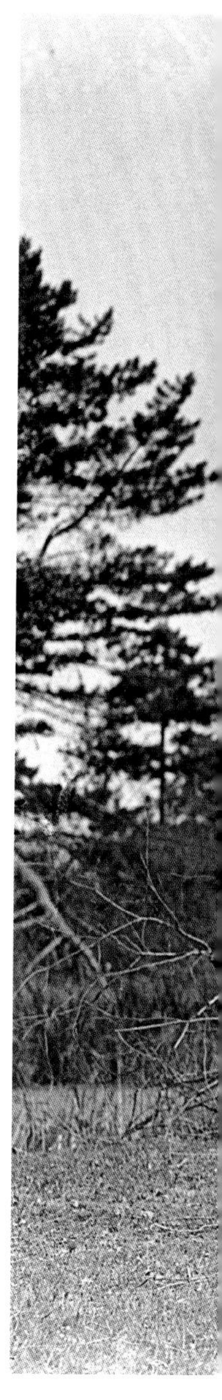

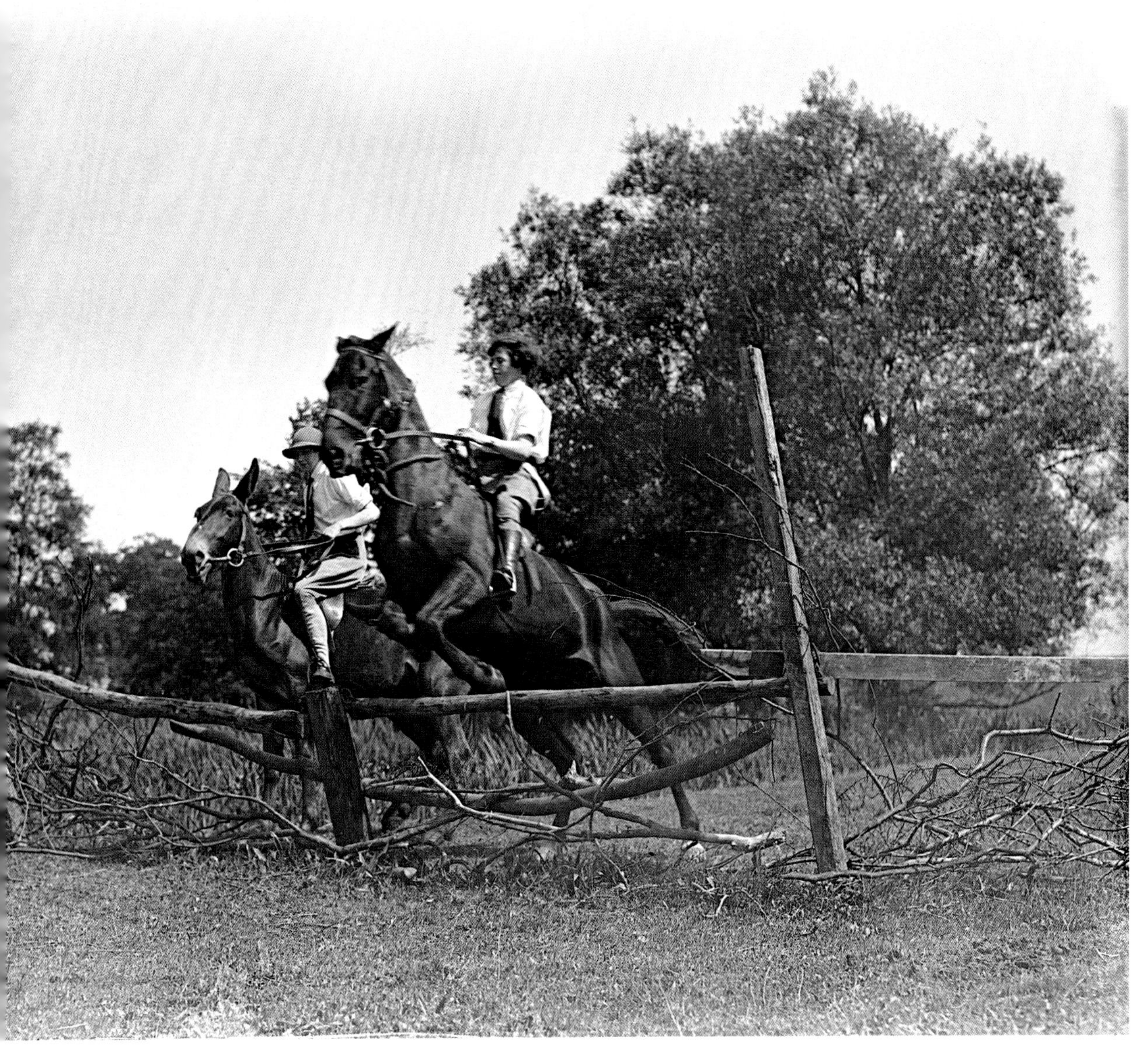

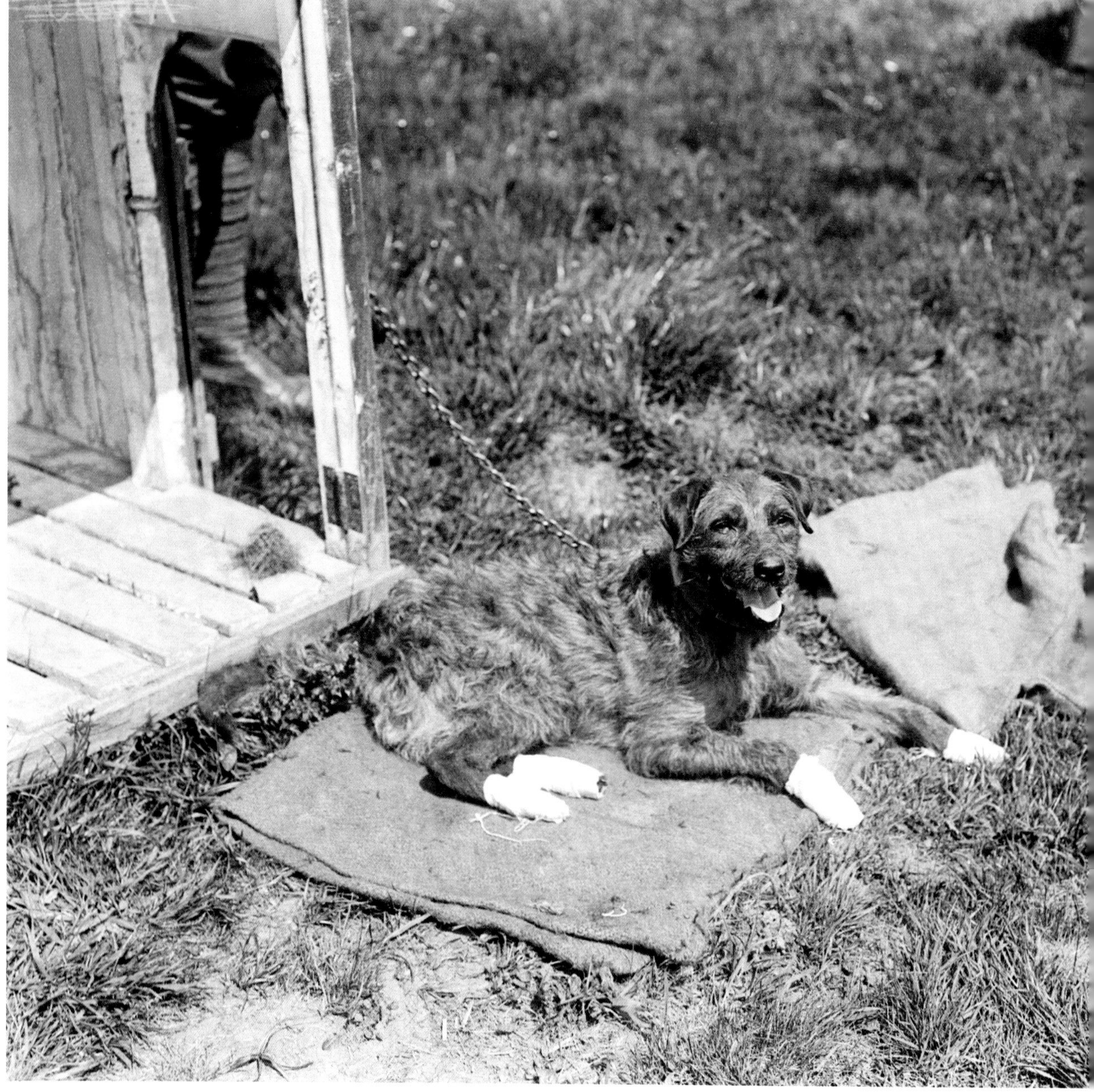

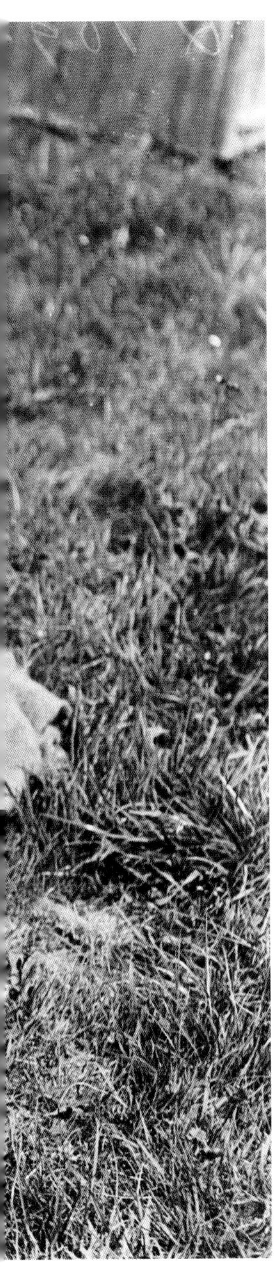

An injured British messenger dog lying on a blanket at the Army Veterinary Corps headquarters kennel near Nieppe Wood, France, May 1918. The dog has bandages on its paws, which were injured after it crossed ground impregnated with mustard gas.

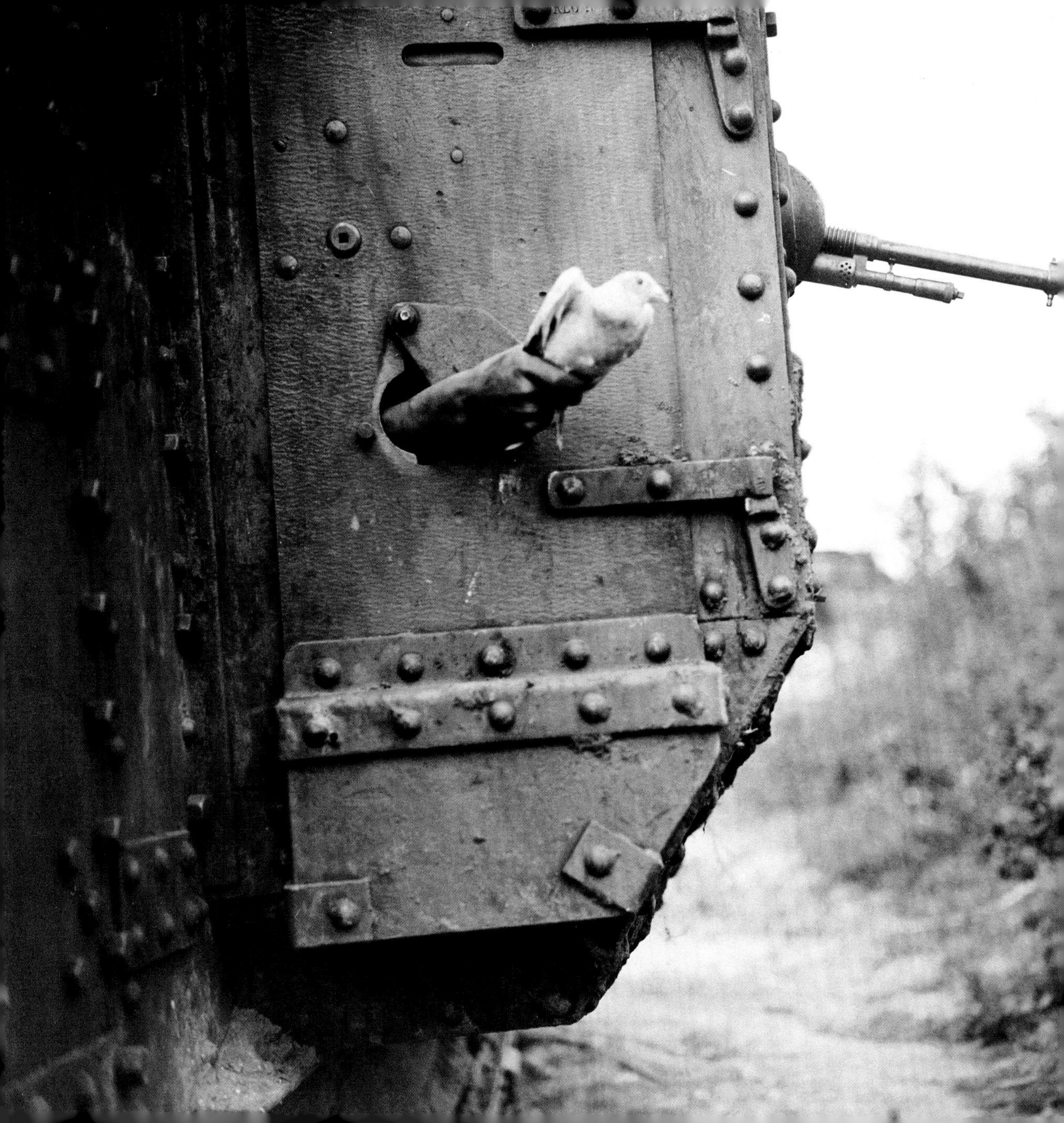

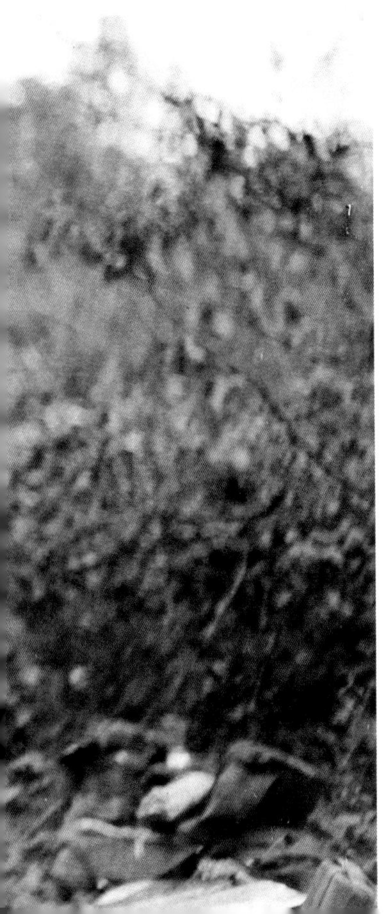

A carrier pigeon being released from a porthole in the side of a Mark V tank, 10th Battalion, Tank Corps, near Albert, France, 9 August 1918, during the Battle of Amiens.

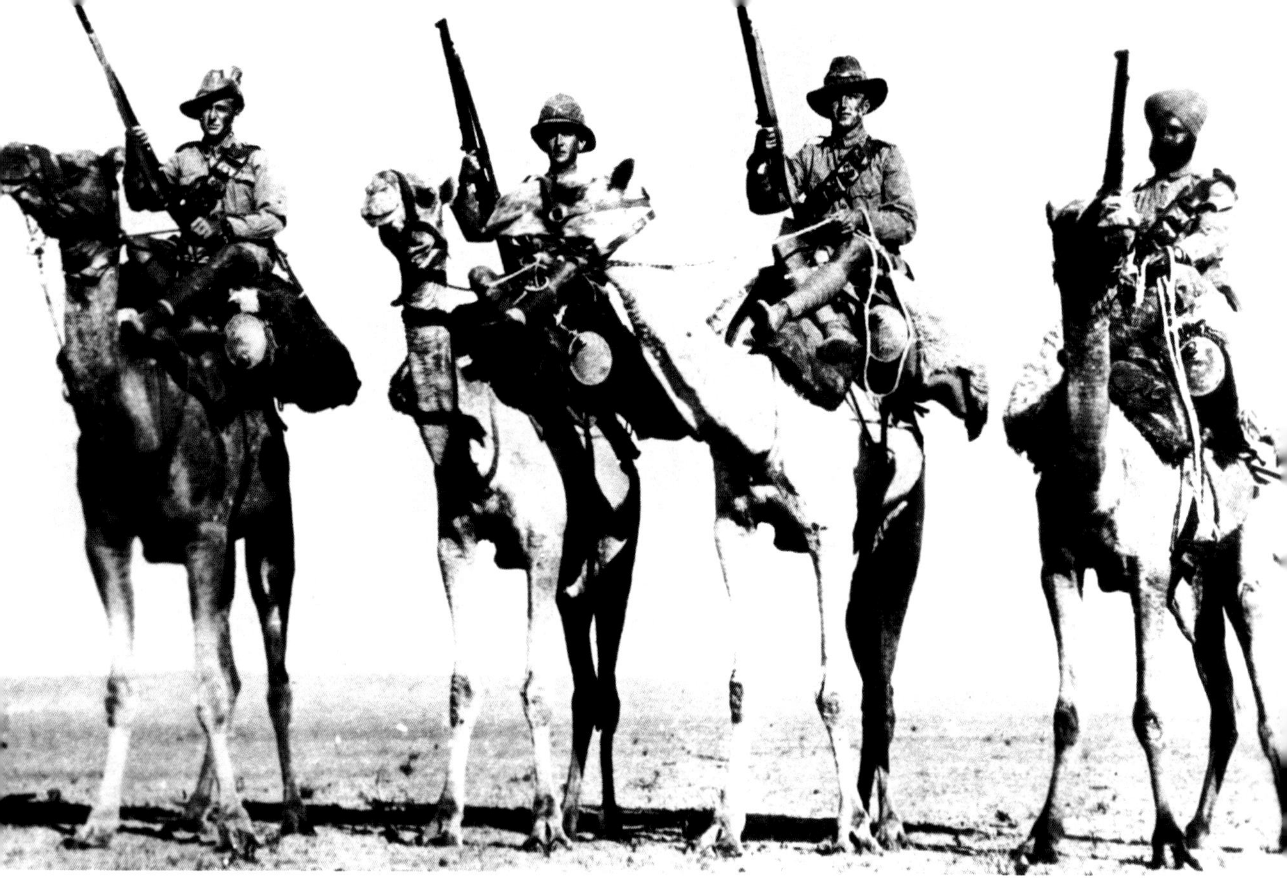

The Imperial Camel Corps in 1918, showing members of the Australian, British, New Zealand and Indian sections. Camels were ideal transport in the Egypt and Palestine campaigns of the First World War.

A pack mule of the 2nd Brigade North Russia Relief Force carrying a 3.7 inch mountain howitzer at Troitsa, Russia, 1919.

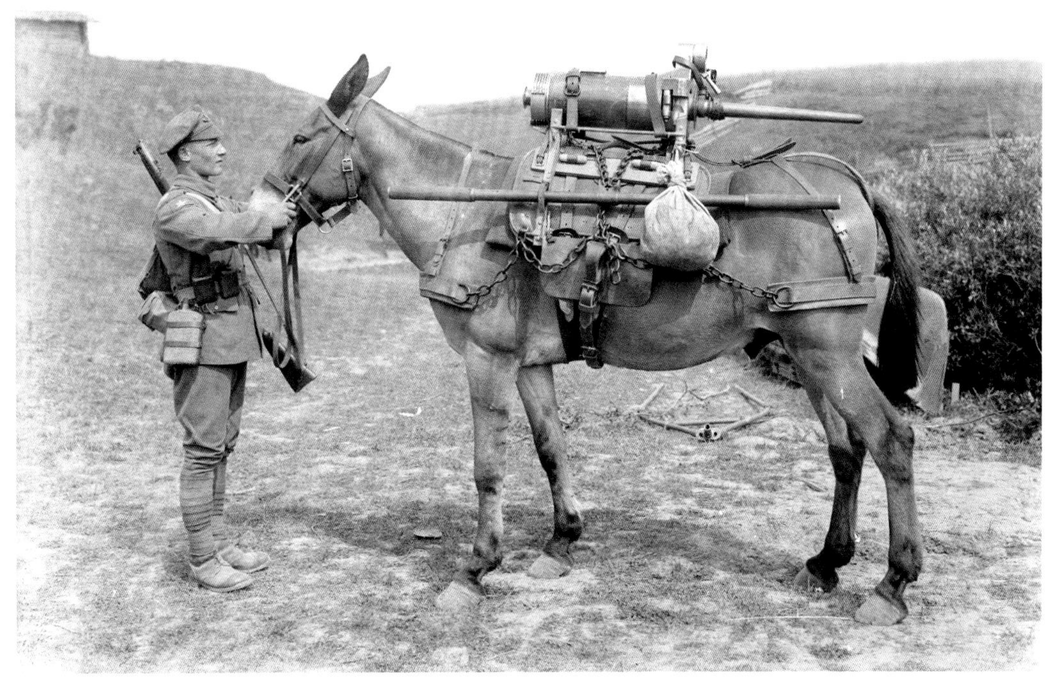

A cow in Essex being painted with white stripes so that it will be visible to motorists during the blackout, September 1939. Motor accidents caused the deaths of many people and animals during the early part of the Second World War.

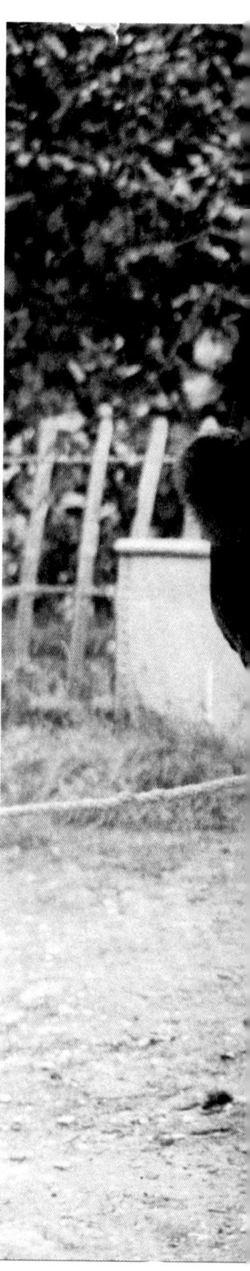

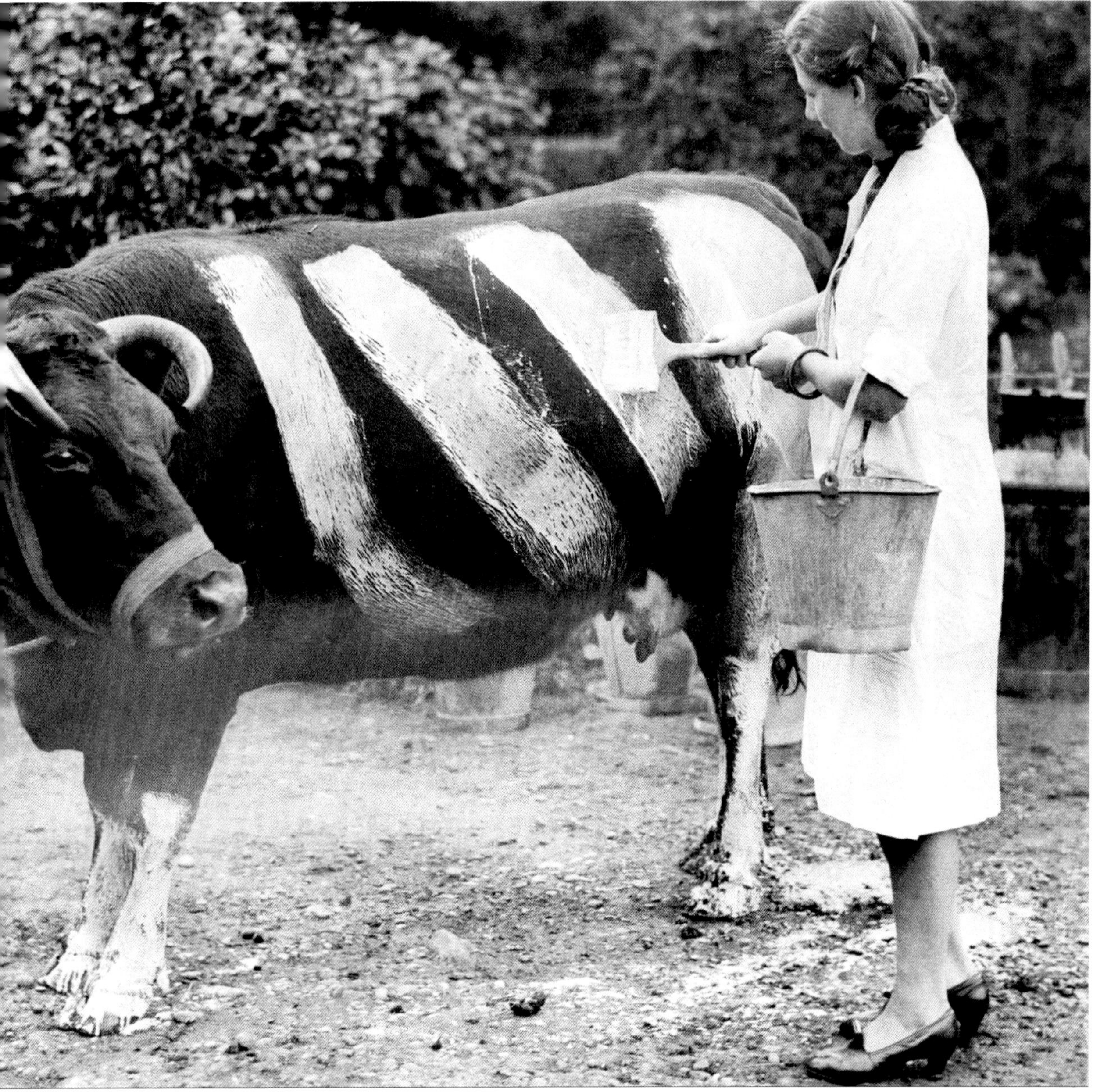

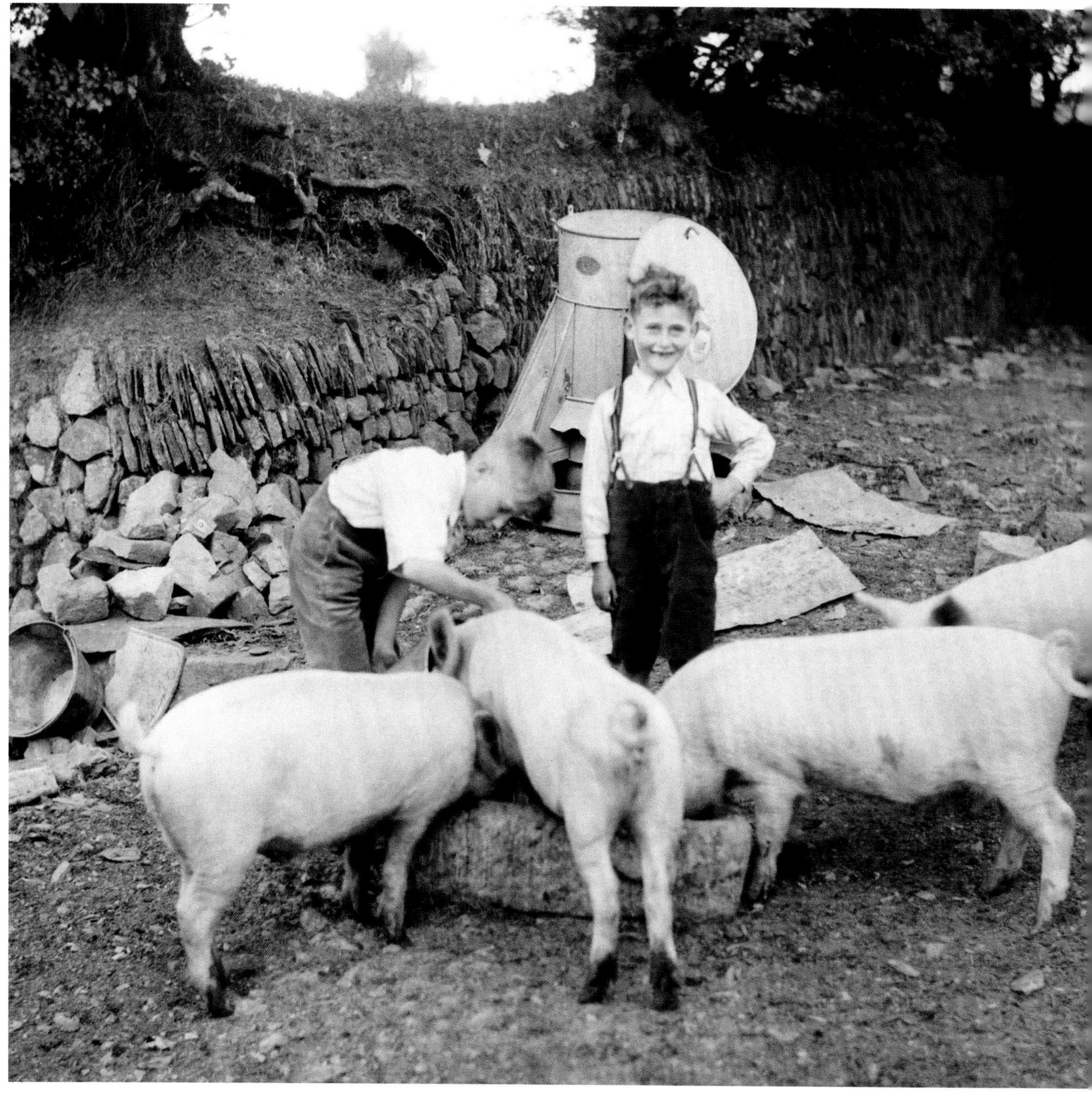

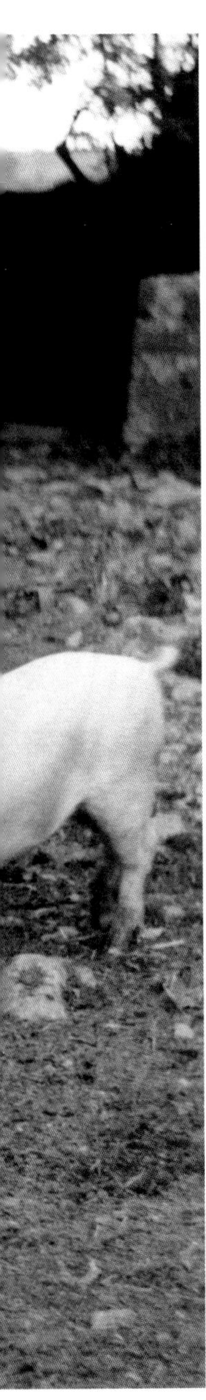

Boys of the Chapman LCC School in Whitechapel, London, feed pigs on a farm in Pembrokeshire, Wales, 1940. For evacuees from cities, this was often their first experience of farm animals.

Two members of the crew of HMS *Hood* with unofficial mascot Bill, a Bull Terrier, 1940. Bill, and his owner, ship's Padre Reverend Harold Beardmore, were transferred off the *Hood* in 1941 shortly before she was sunk in action.

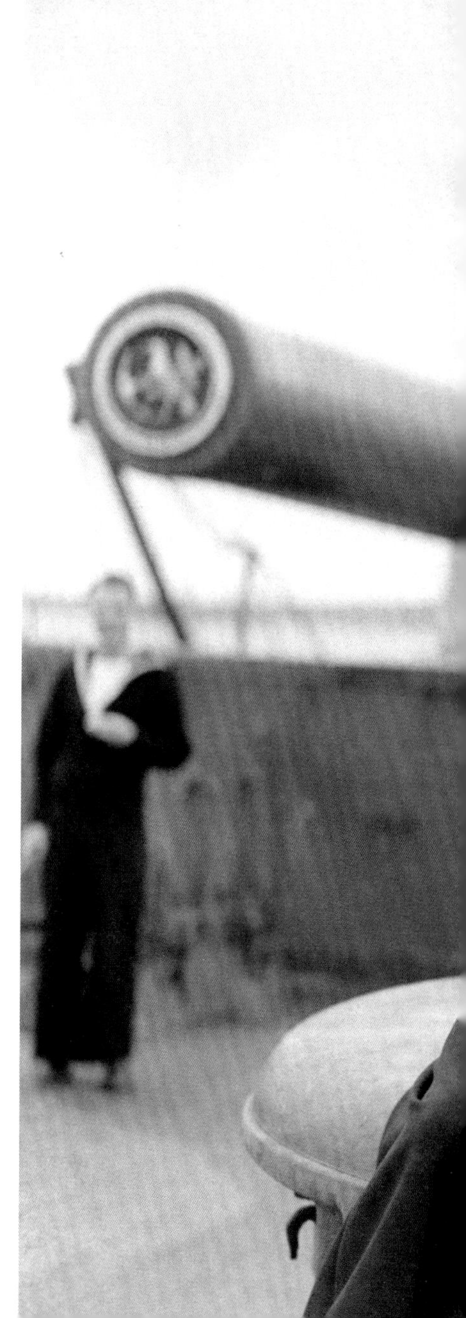

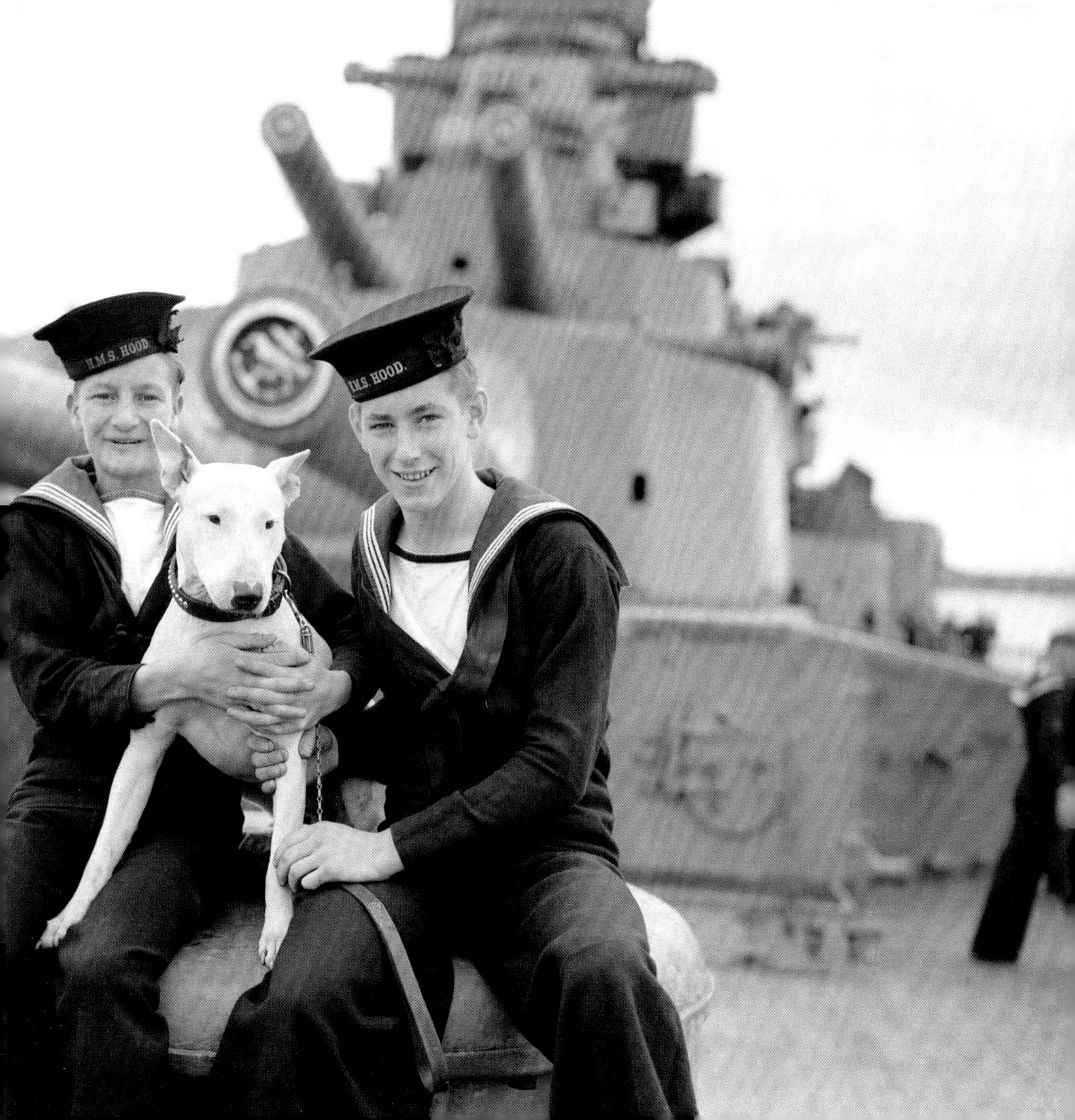
H.M.S. HOOD.
H.M.S. HOOD.

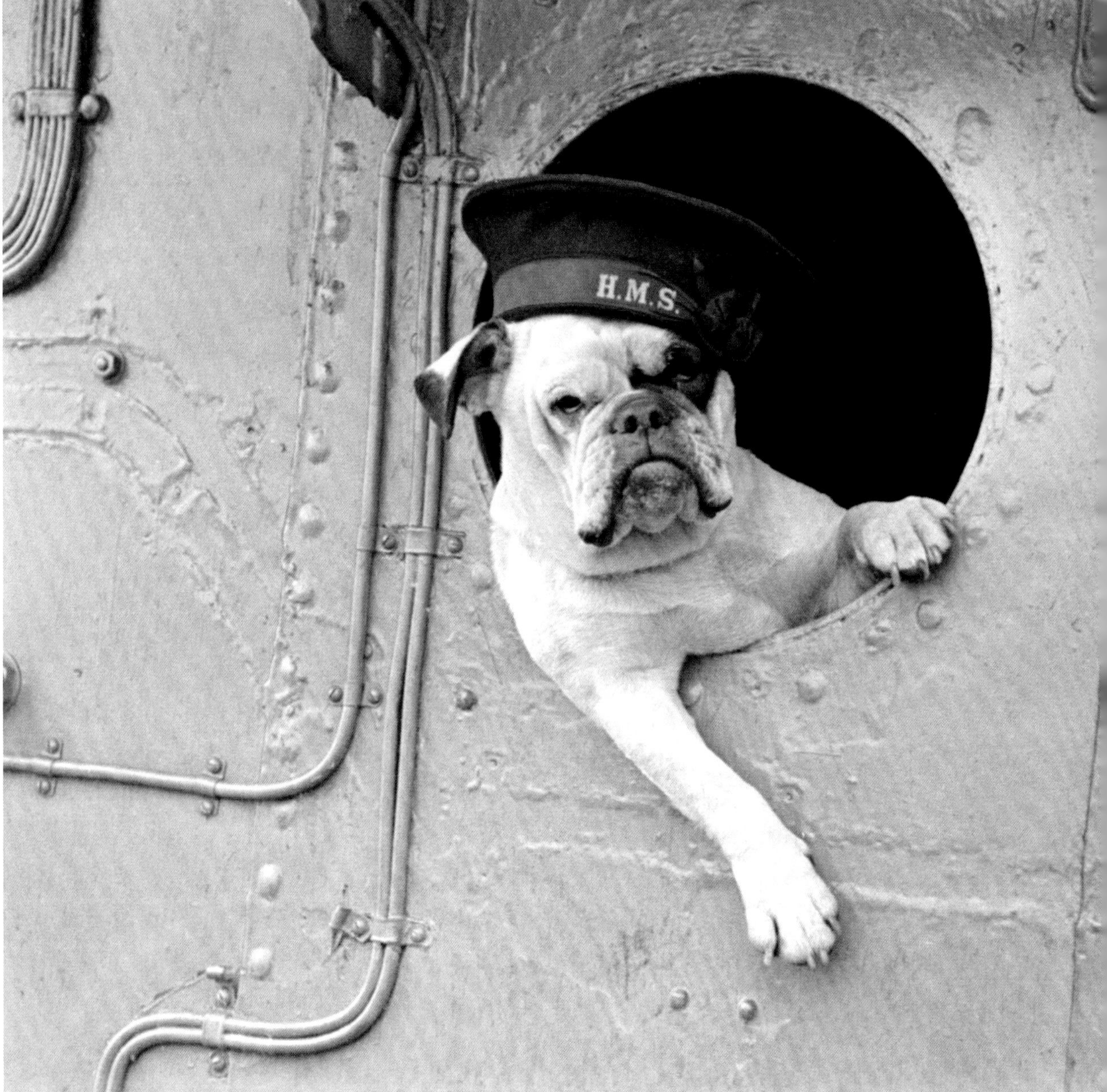
H.M.S.

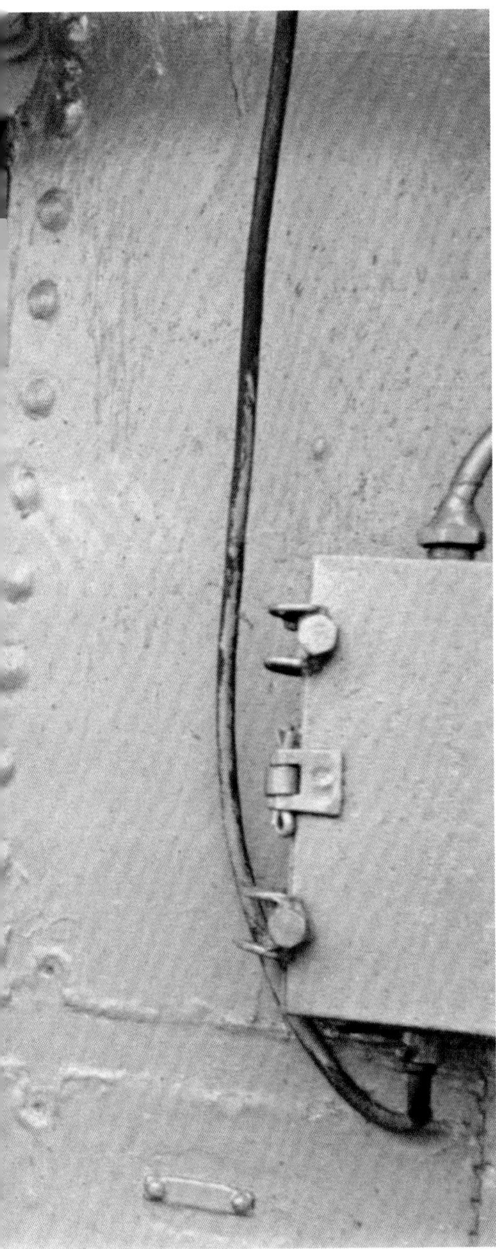

Venus, the Bulldog mascot of the destroyer HMS *Vansittart*, 1940. Bulldogs were popular mascots not only for representing the British 'Bulldog spirit', but also for their supposed resemblance to Prime Minister Winston Churchill.

Two Canadian soldiers strap a basket to the back of an Airedale Terrier during a training exercise in Britain, 1940. The basket contains carrier pigeons. A quarter of a million pigeons were used by the British during the Second World War.

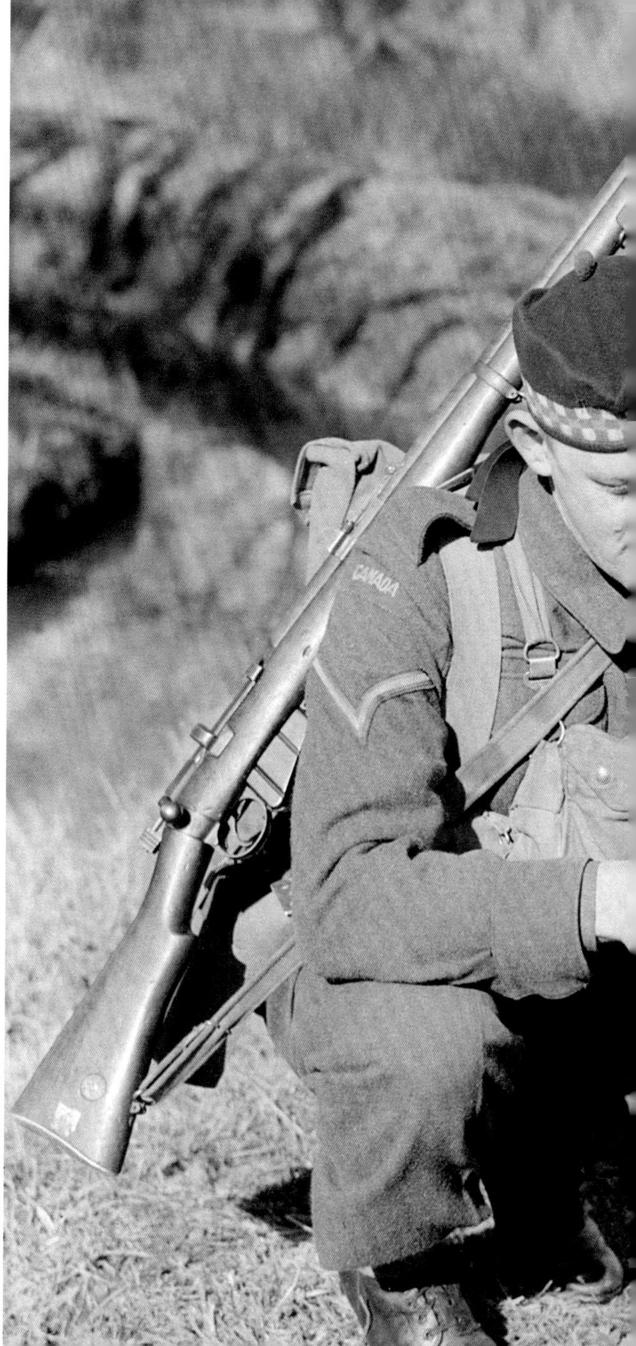

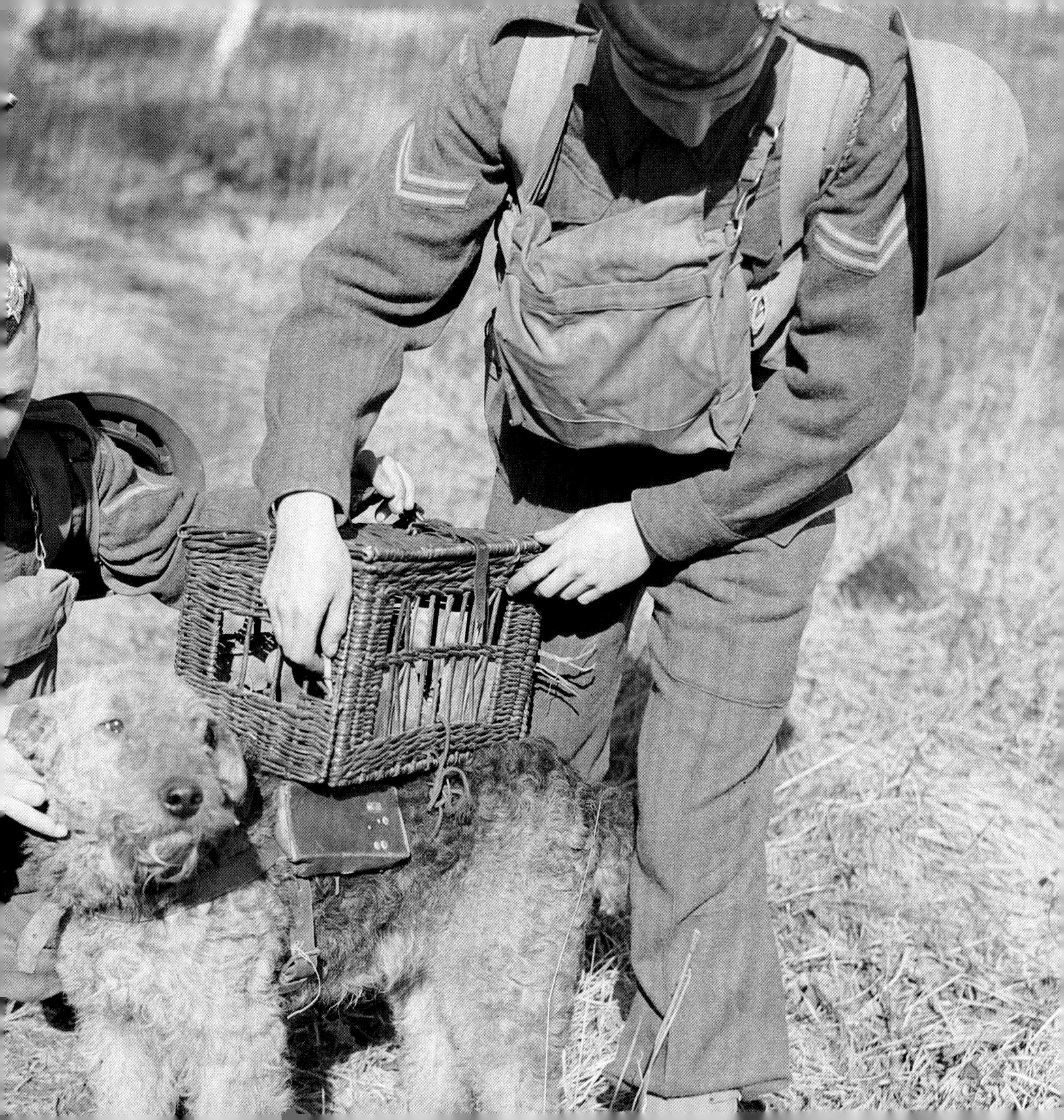

An Indian soldier in France fitting a gas mask on a mule, 21 February 1940. Luckily gas was not used on the battlefield during the Second World War. Animals often thought they were food bags, and many gas masks were chewed to the point of uselessness.

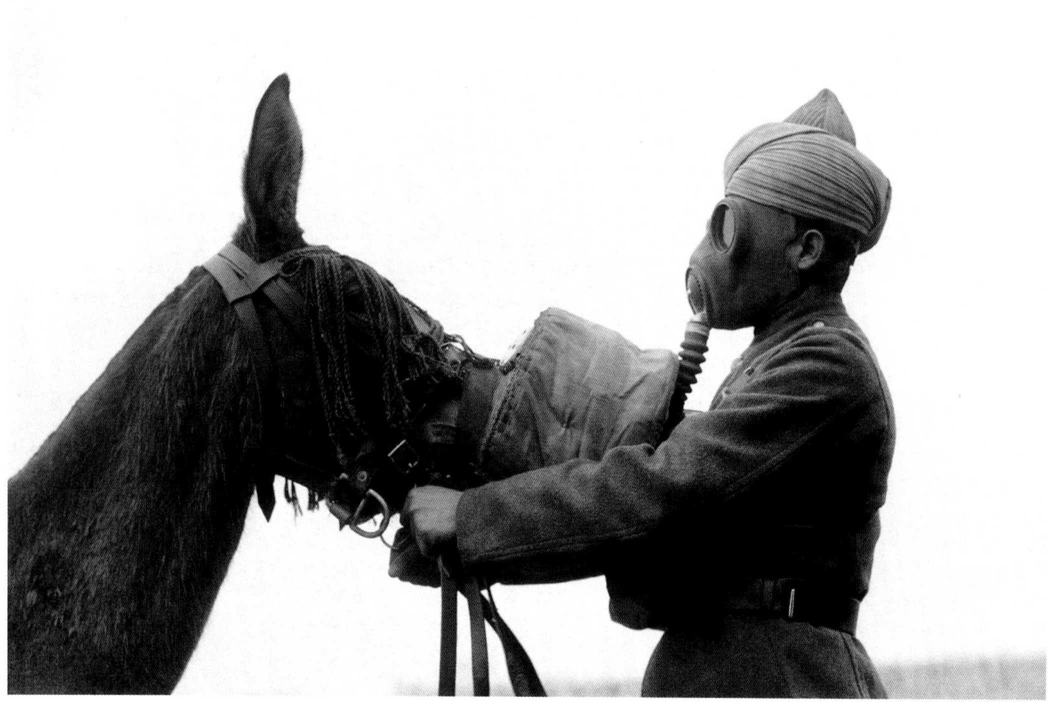

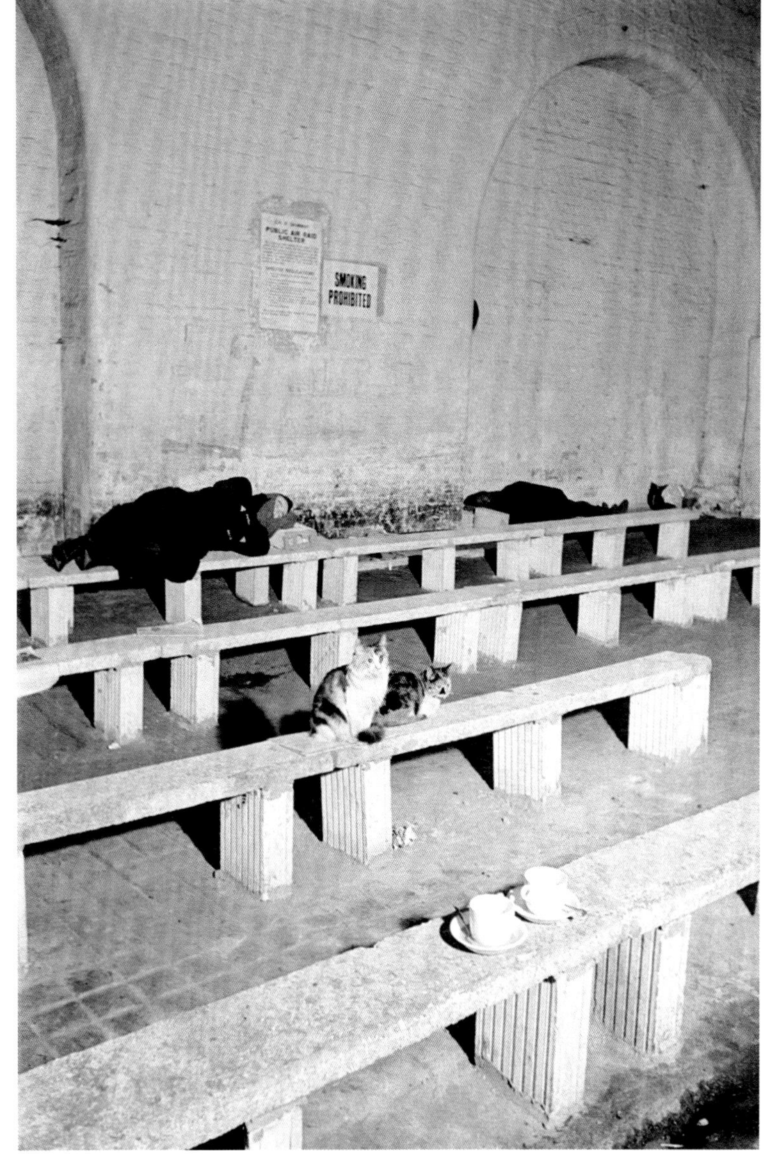

Two cats take residence on benches under railway arches used as a public air raid shelter for dispossessed people in west London, 1940. Although public shelters weren't meant for pets, many were still brought, or snuck, in.

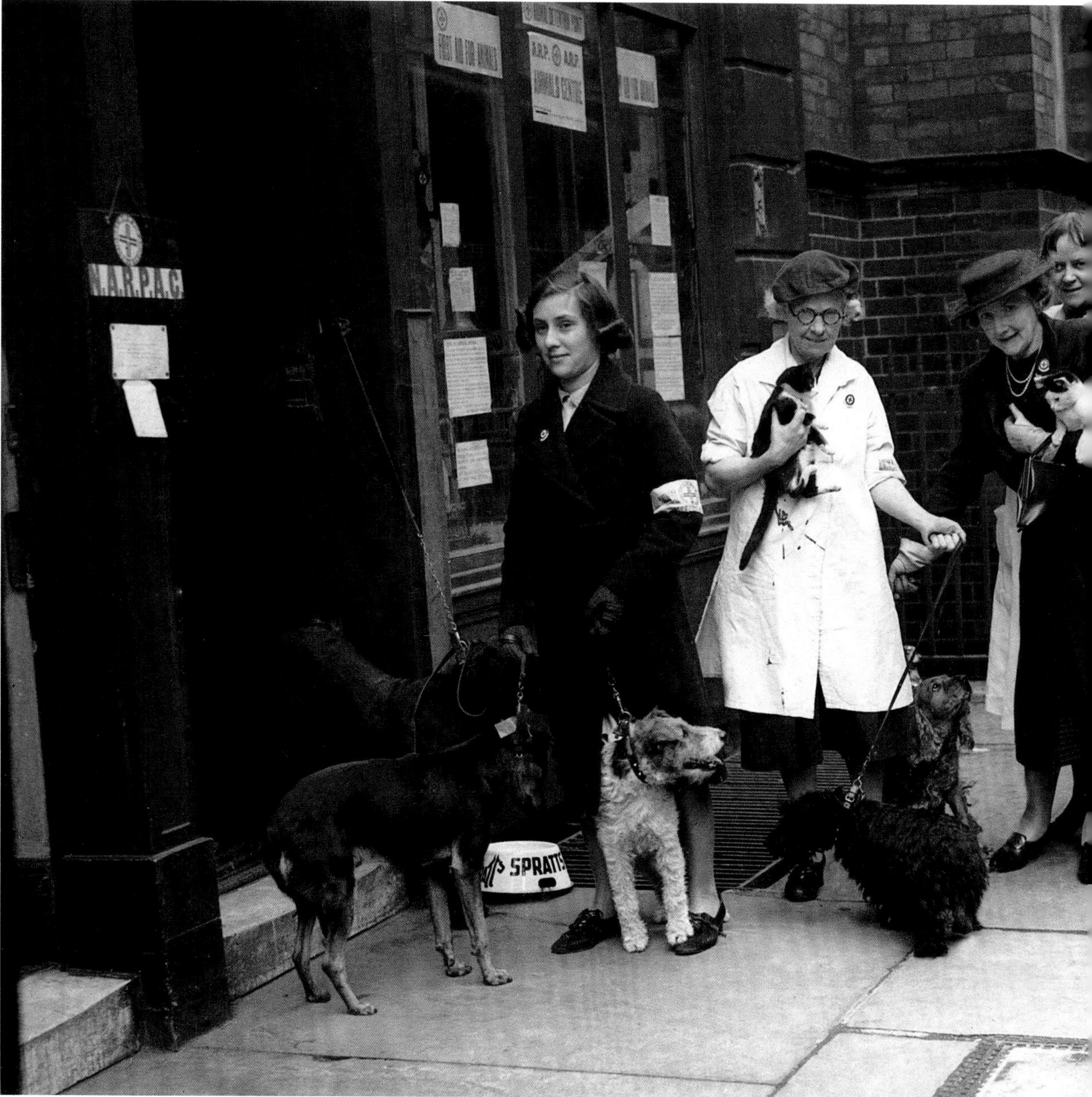
FIRST AID FOR ANIMALS
N.A.R.P.A.C
SPRATTS

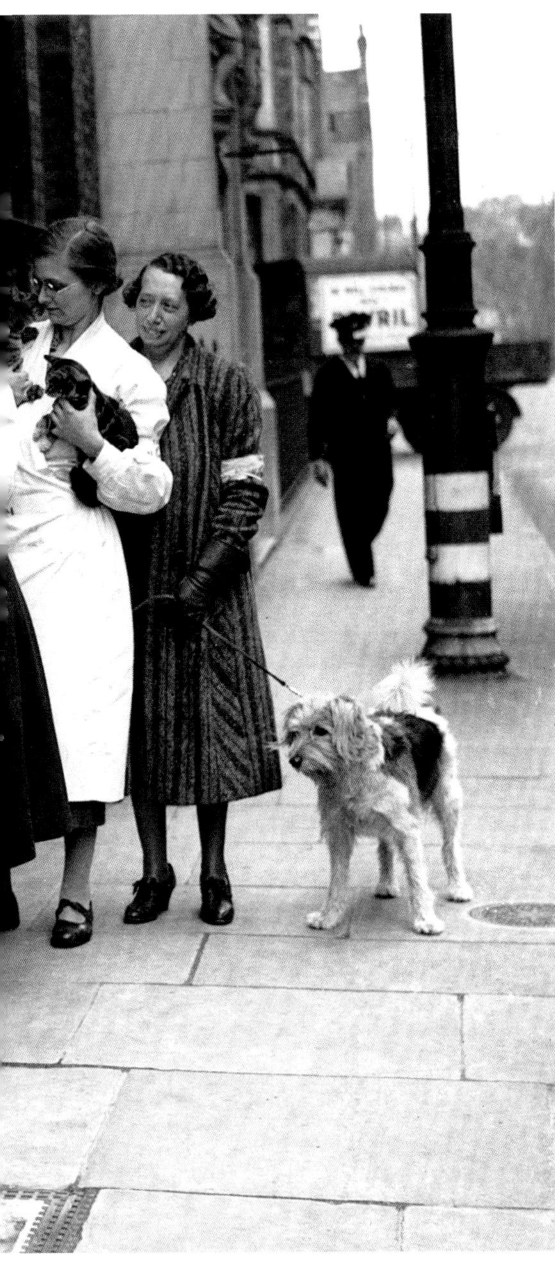

The National Air Raid Precautions Animals Committee (NARPAC) looked after animals that had been left homeless after enemy bombing. Here, helpers with cats and dogs from bombed homes arrive at an NARPAC centre at Torrington Place, London, October 1940.

A member of the Women's Land Army (WLA) with two shire horses harrowing a field in Surrey, 1941. Farming was vital for supplying the country with food, and at its peak in 1944, there were 80,000 members of the WLA.

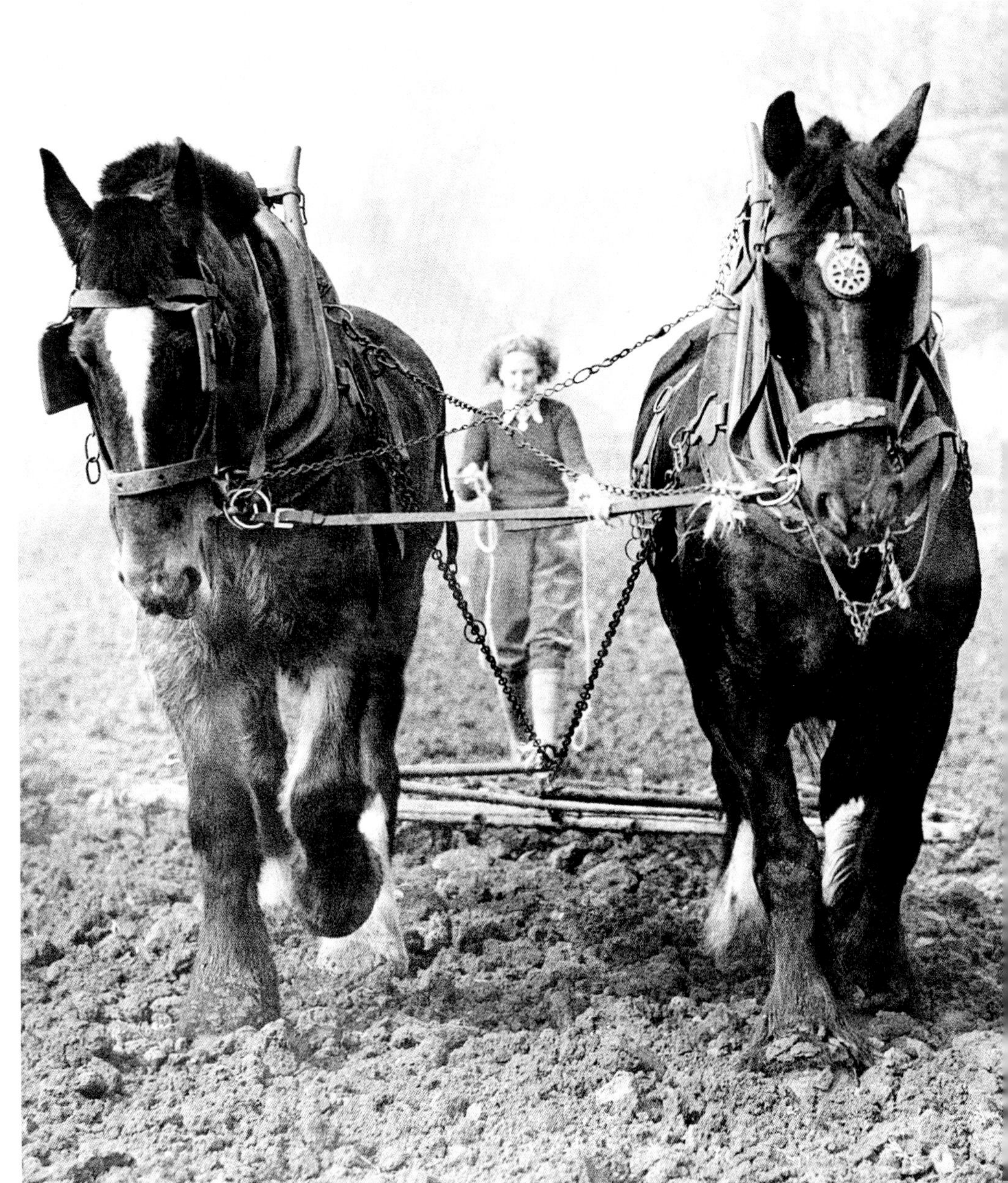

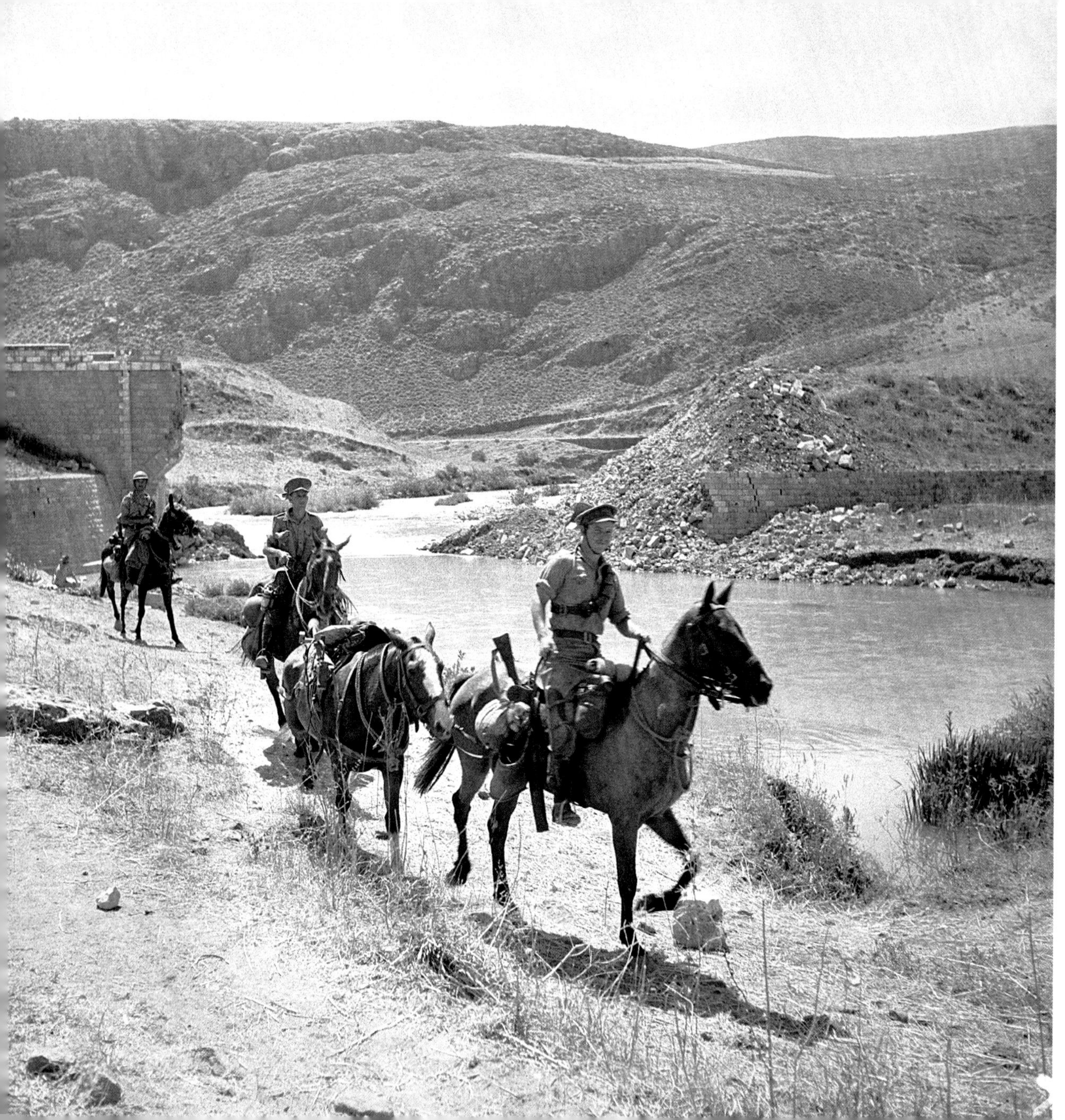

The Cheshire Yeomanry patrolling on horseback in Syria, June 1941. At the outbreak of the Second World War the British Army and its Empire troops only had a small number of mounted units. British cavalry horses saw action in the Middle East between 1940 and1942, where they were used for patrol and reconnaissance work.

Troops of the Royal Army Service Corps putting Lewis gun ammunition into the pack carried by Alsatian Mark, at work with British troops in Eastern Command, August 1941. Mark was given to the British Expeditionary Force by the 1st French Army in 1939.

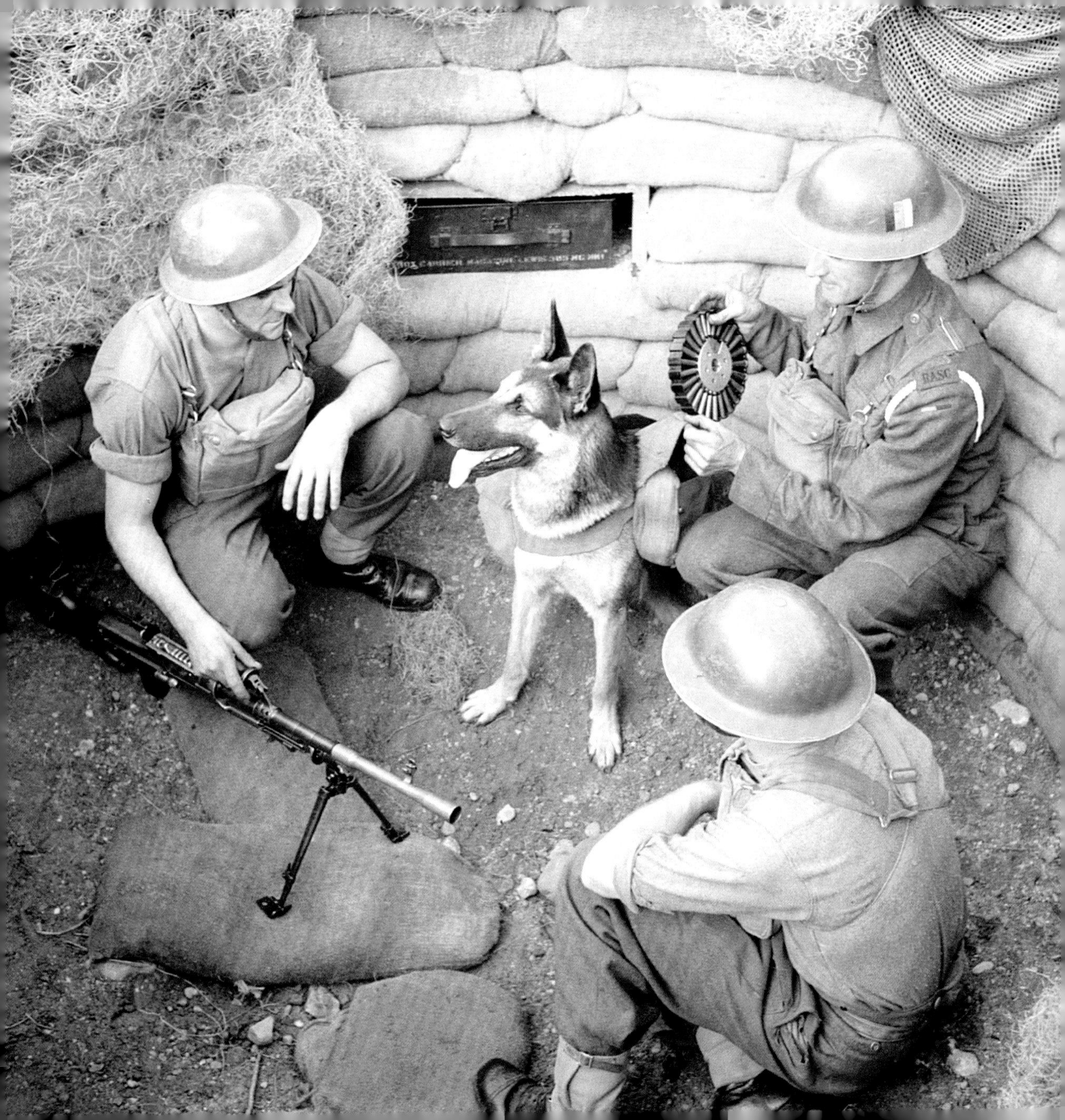
RASC

Air Raid Precautions (ARP) dog Rip sits on rubble following an air raid in Poplar, London, August 1941. Picked up as a stray by an ARP Warden, E King, he is credited with saving the lives of over 100 people. Rip became one of eight dogs on the home front to win the Dickin Medal for bravery.

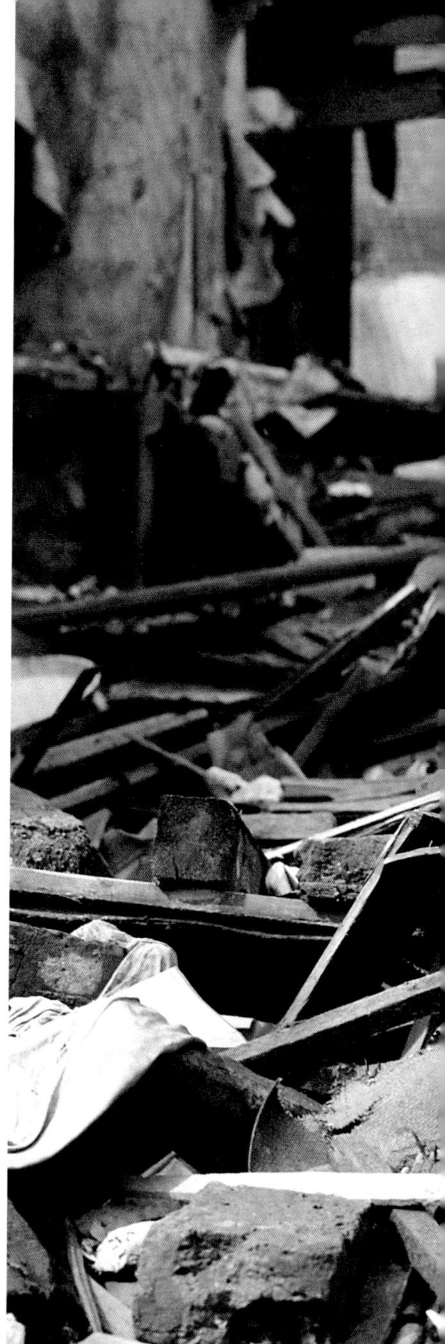

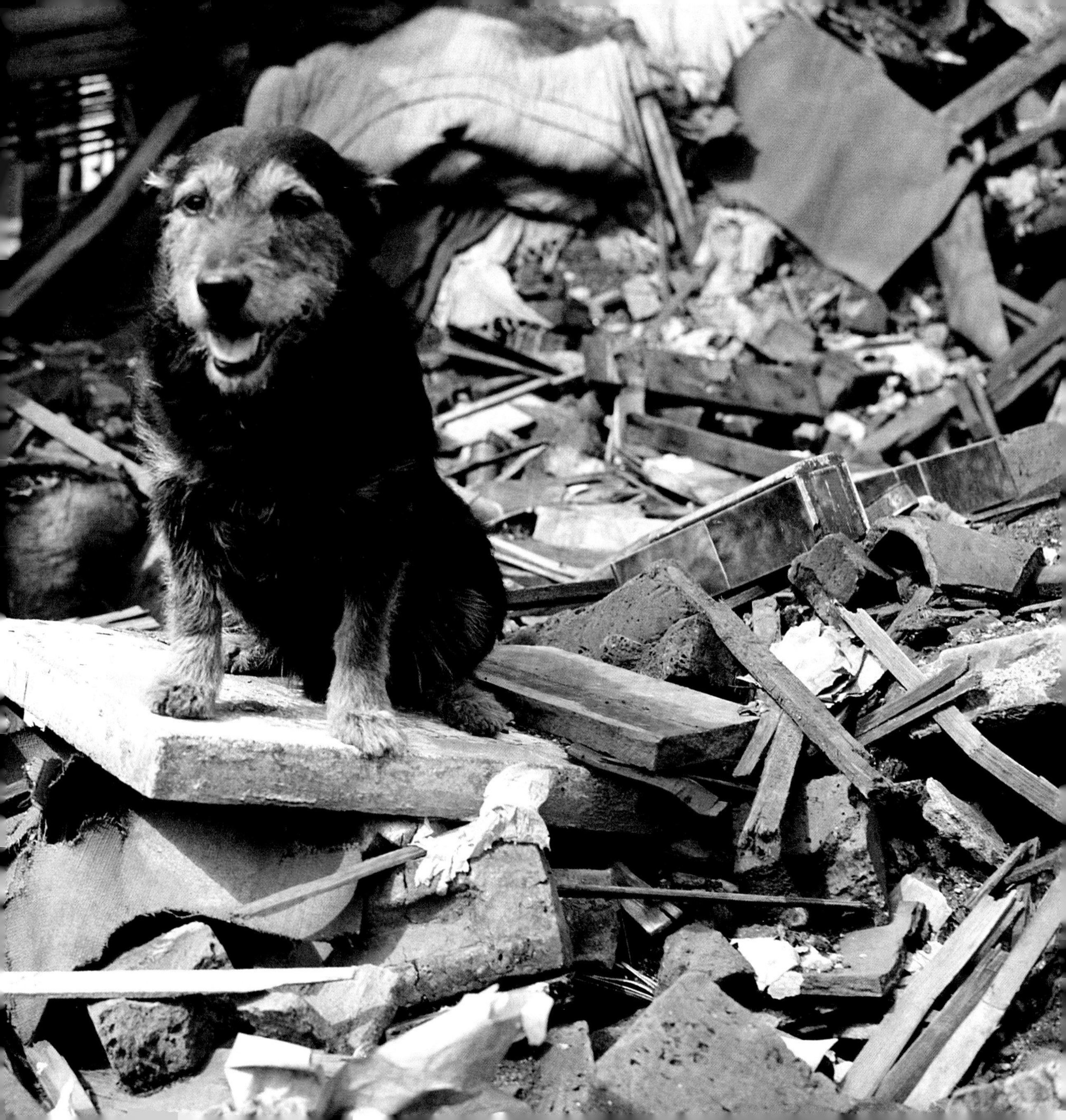

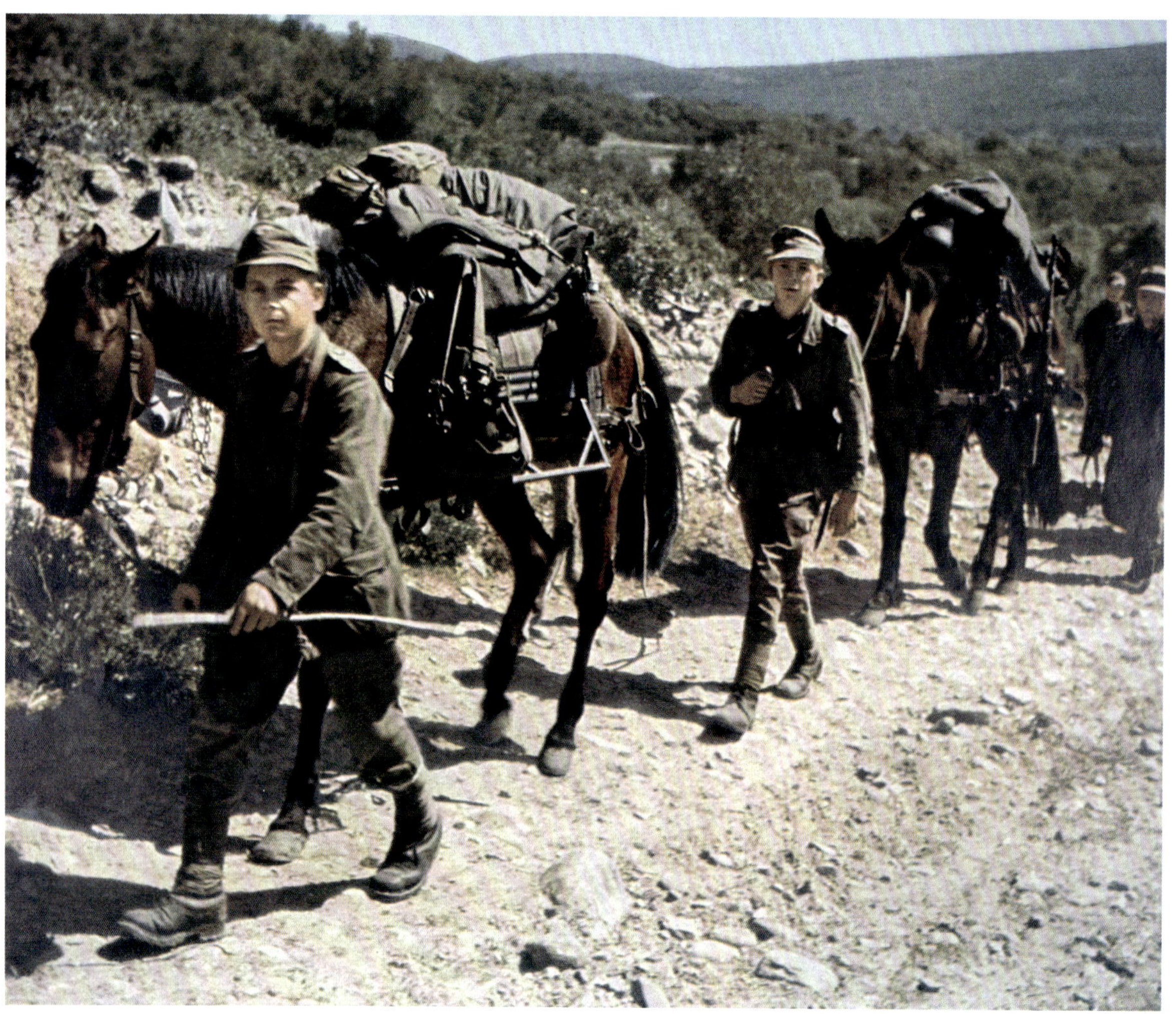

German *Gebirgsjäger* [mountain troops] with their pack animals in Italy or the Balkans, 1941–1942. Unlike the Allied armies, and despite its revolutionary use of tanks and aircraft, the German Army was still largely horse based throughout the Second World War.

Winkie the pigeon was awarded the Dickin Medal for helping in the recovery of these airmen, when she flew over 120 miles to alert rescue services that their Beaufighter had crashed in the North Sea in February 1943.

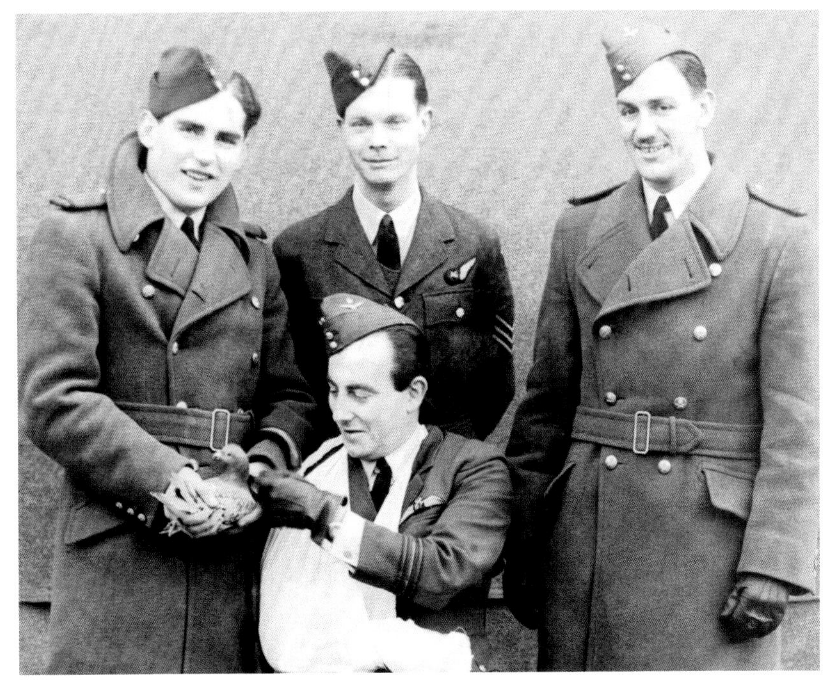

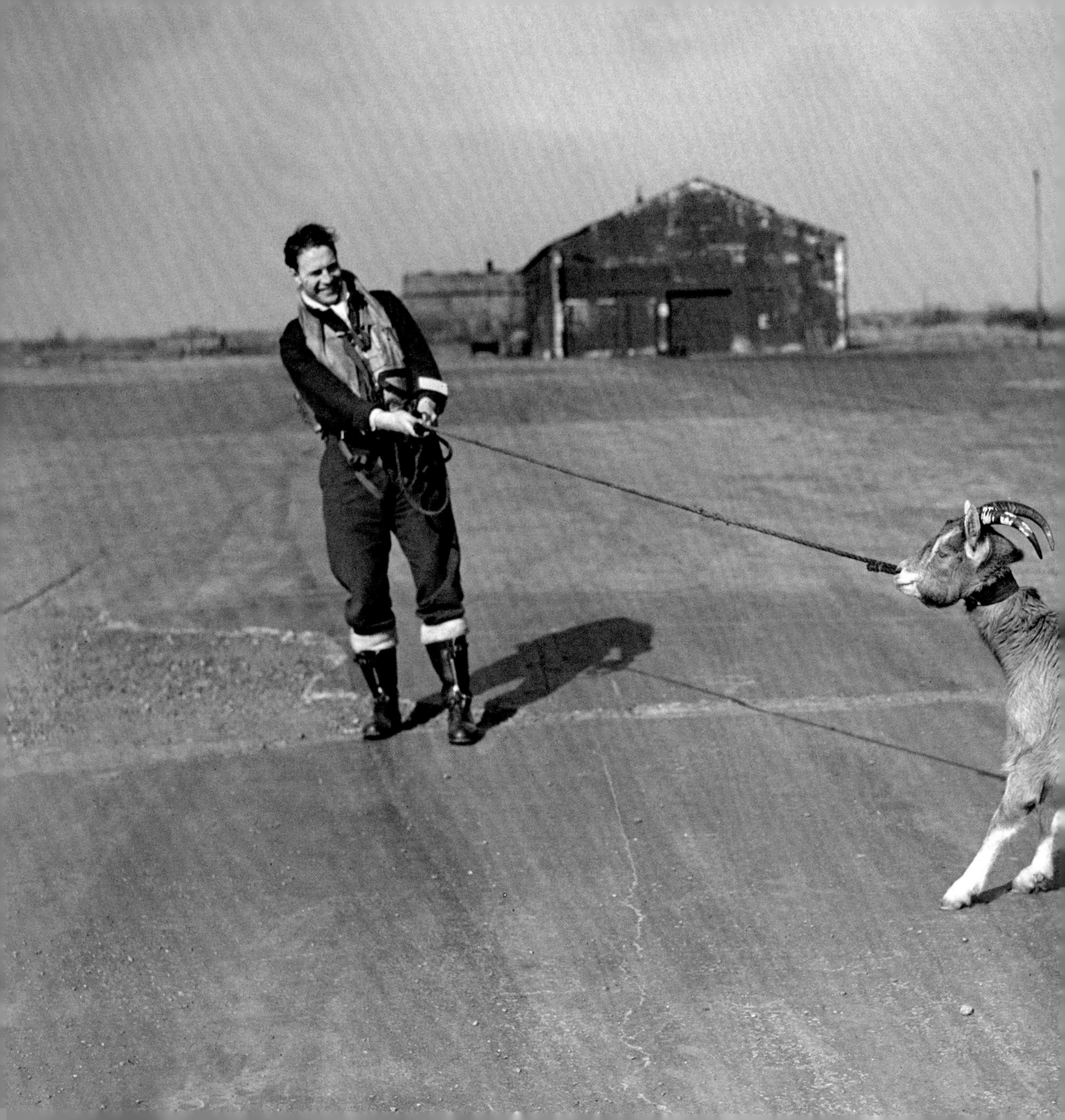

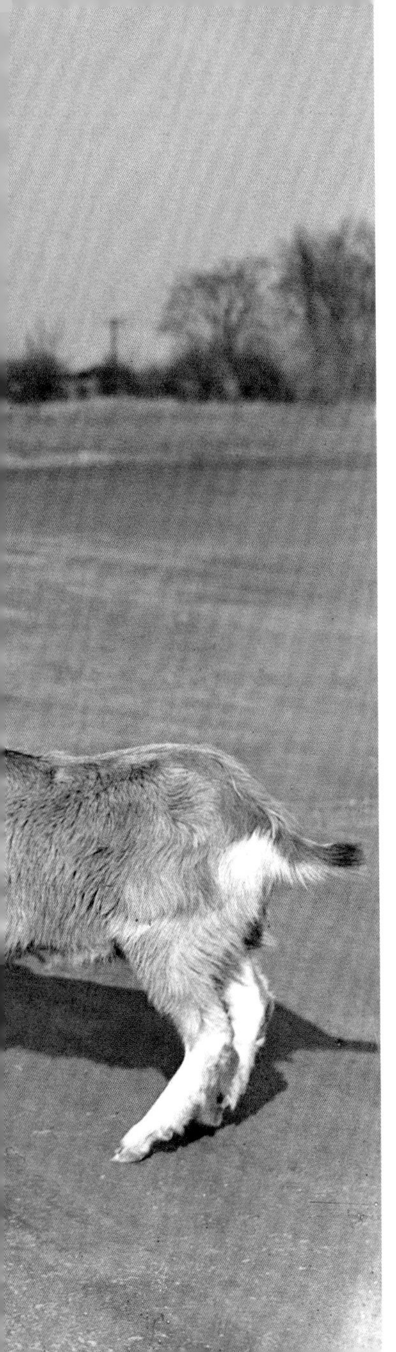

Wing-Commander Billy, the goat mascot of the Royal Air Force fighter station at Manston, 'pulls rank' over Flying Officer Peter Edward Raw, a Typhoon pilot of No. 609 Squadron, wishing to take him for a walk, 8 March 1943. William 'Billy' de Goat ended the war as an honorary Group Captain. F/O Raw was killed in the Netherlands in 1944.

Mister, half Chow Chow, half police hound, in a US Army Eighth Air Force flying fortress with his owner Sergeant Harold Rogers DFC, July 1943. Sergeant Rogers designed the respirator worn by Mister. Together they made 25 missions, once bailing out over the North Sea. Mister survived the war, but Sergeant Rogers was killed during his second tour.

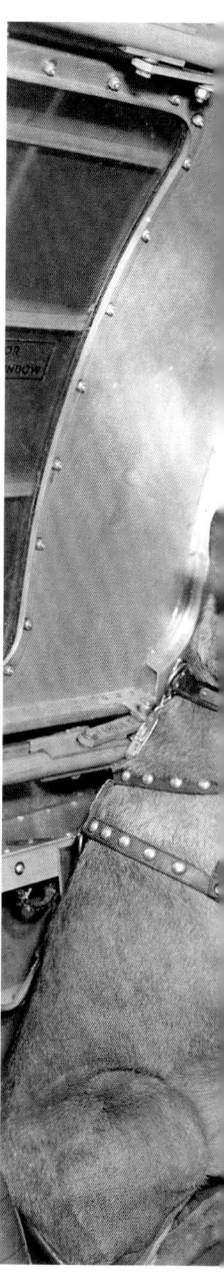

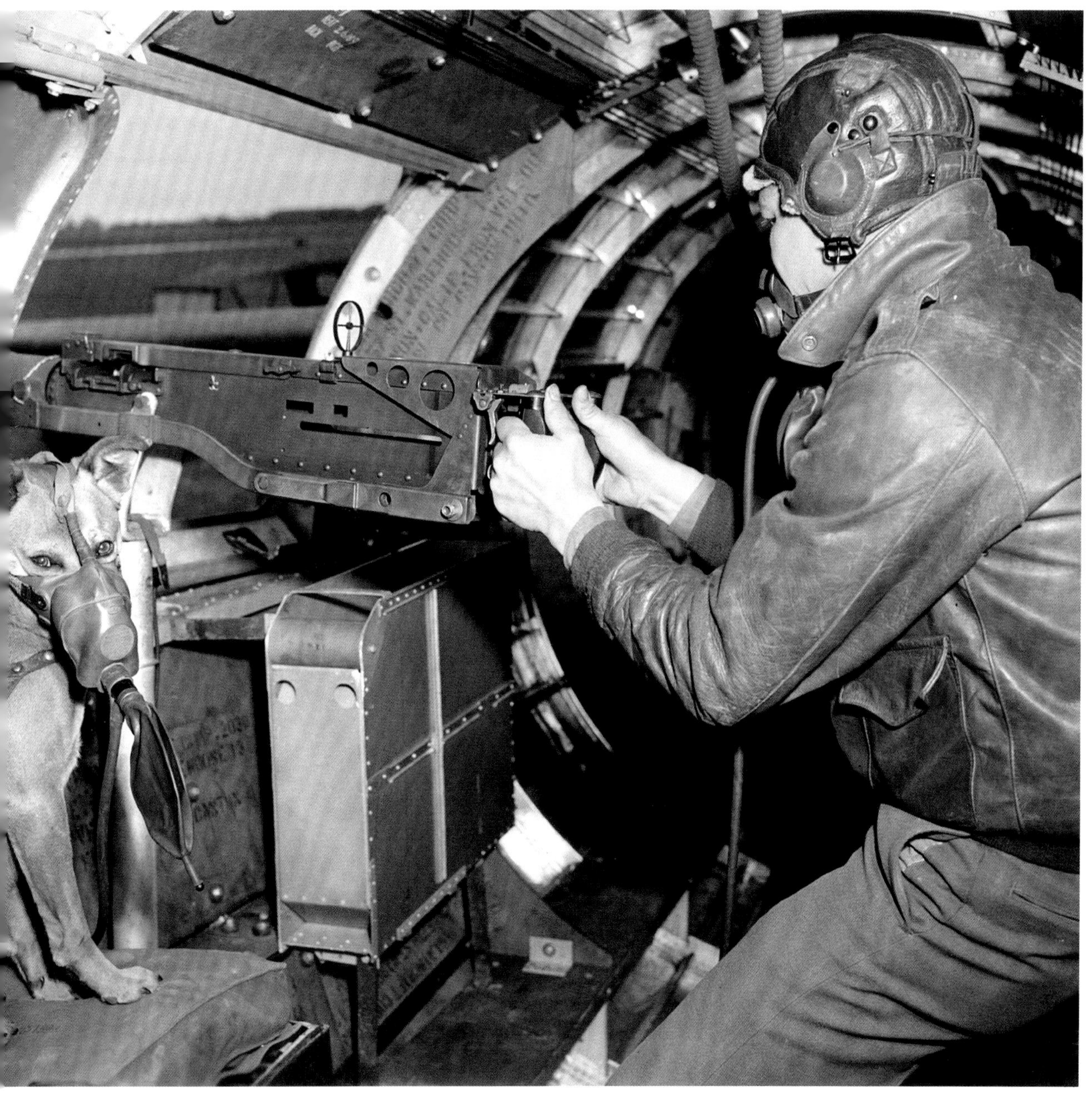

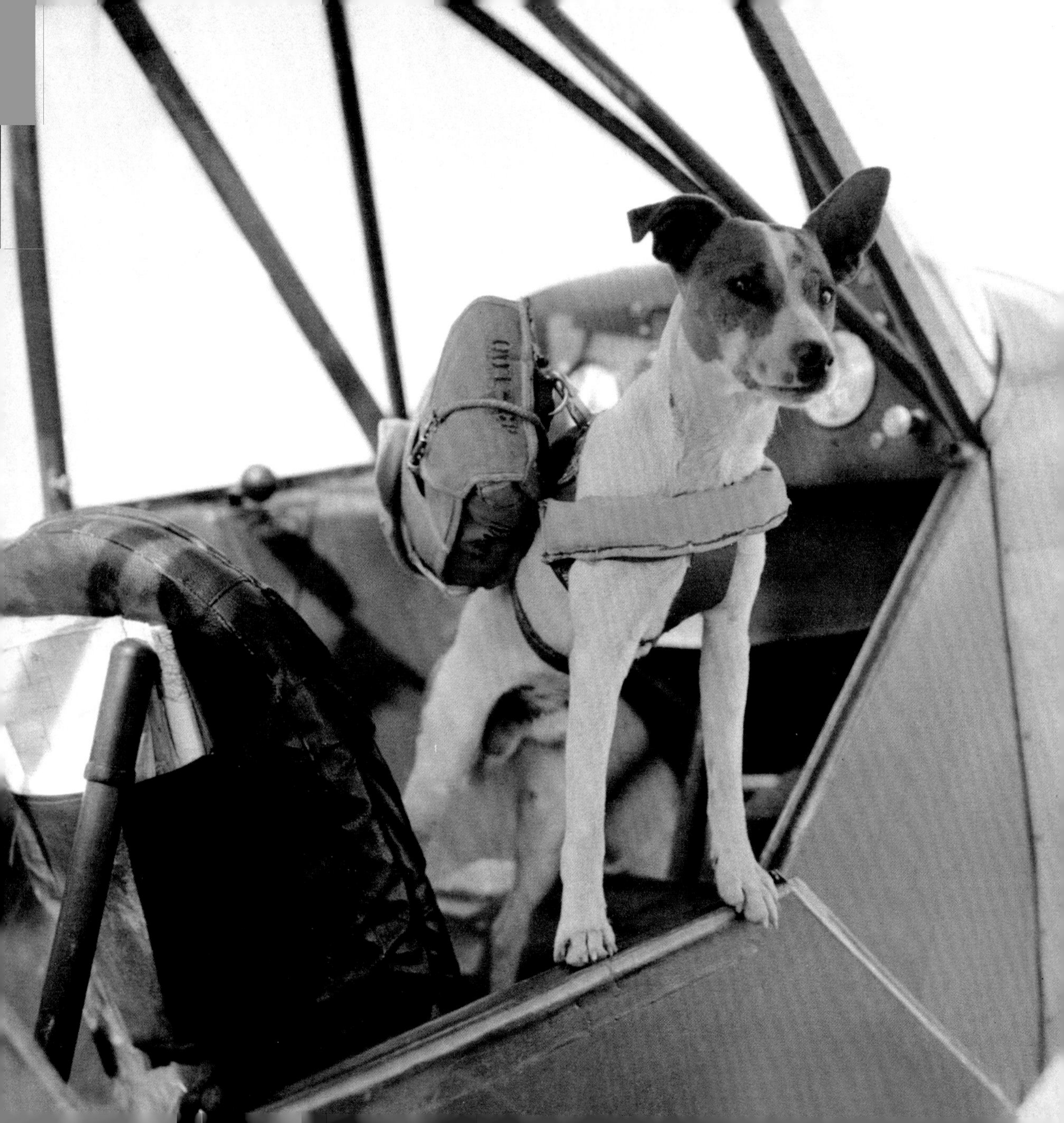

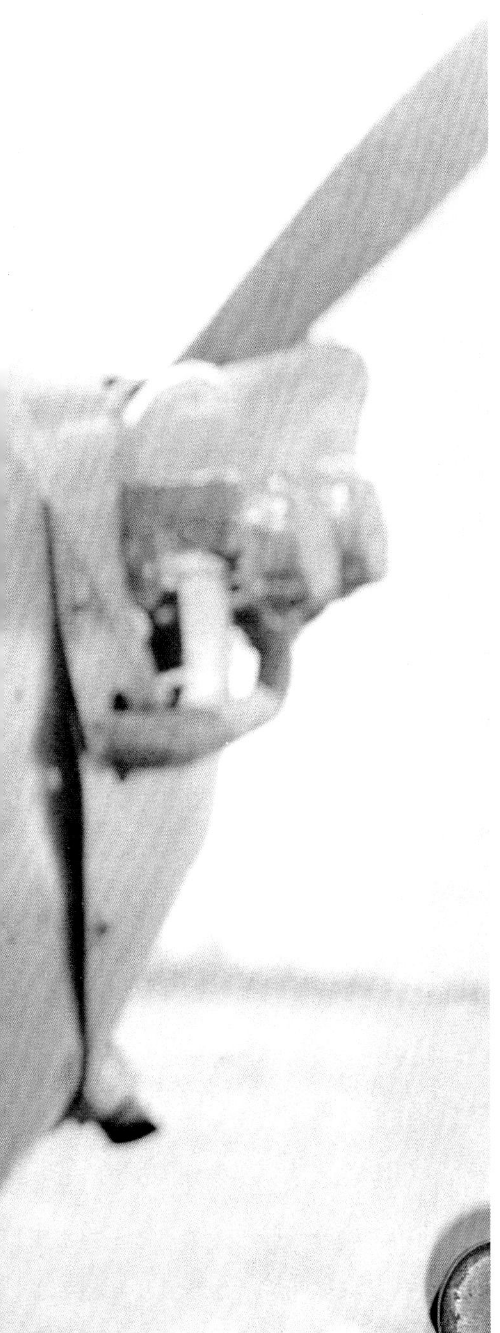

Salvo, the first dog in the United States Air Force in Britain to become a parachute jumper ('Paradog'). In 1943 he practised leaping from 1,500 feet at Andrews Field, near Great Saling, Essex, to be used as a dispatch carrier for his master, Lieutenant Hugh Fletcher.

Flight Sergeant James Hyde, a fighter pilot serving with No.132 Squadron, Royal Air Force, pictured by a Supermarine Spitfire with Dingo, the squadron commander's pet dog, at Detling, Kent, December 1943.

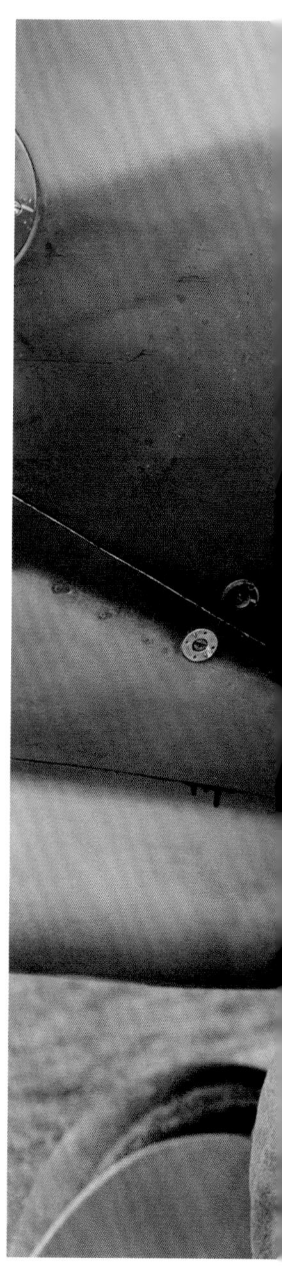

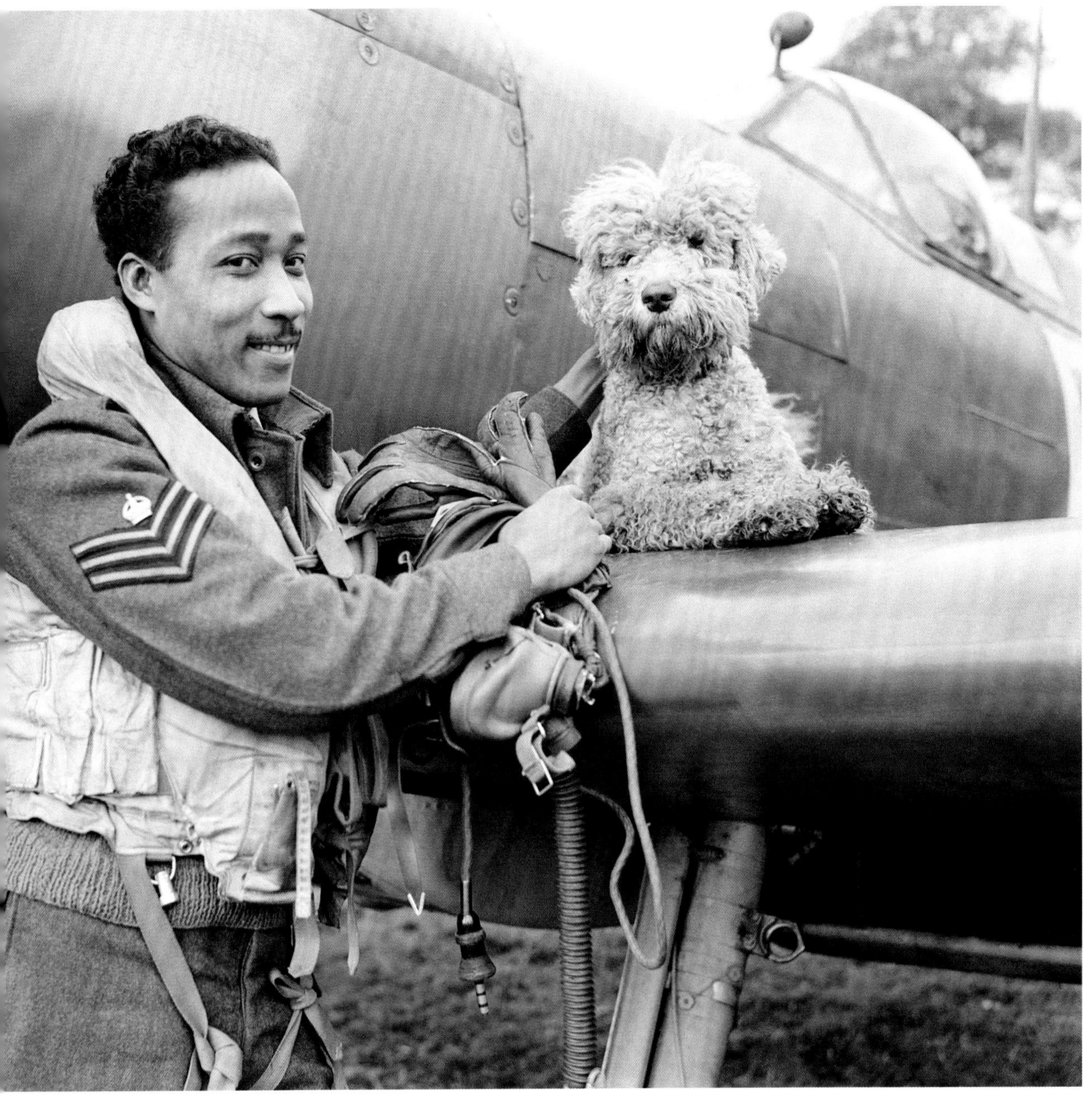

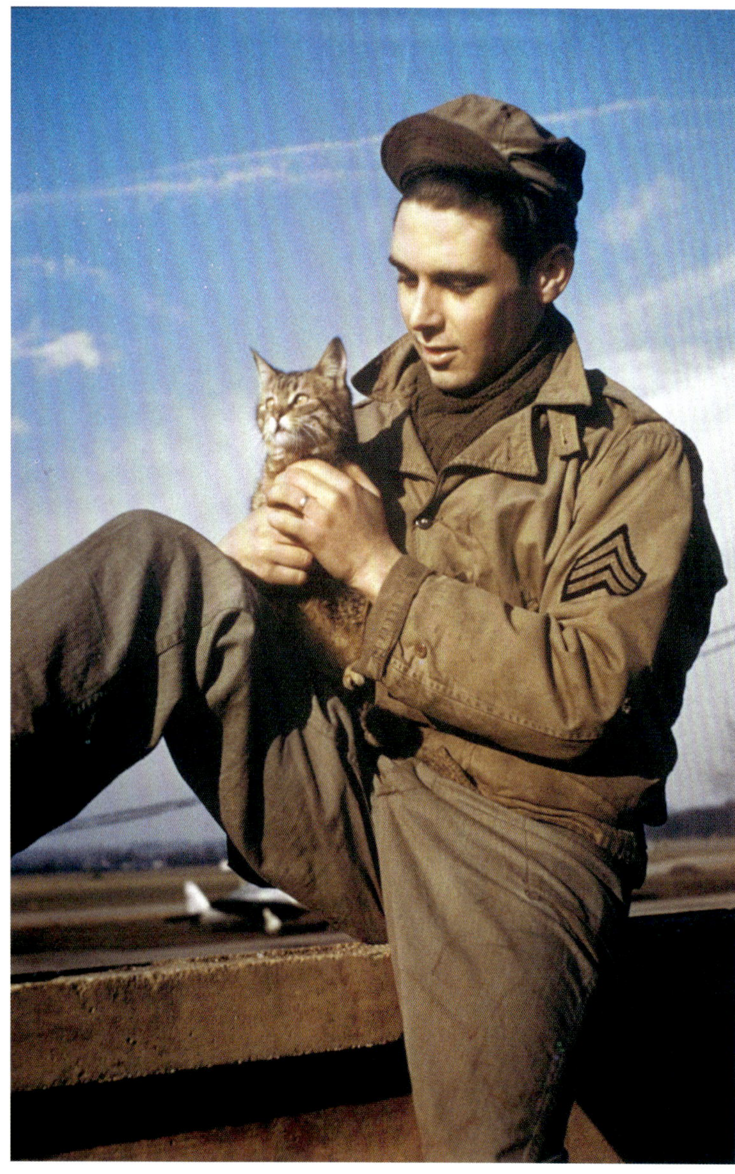

'Cross Eyes' the cat, a mascot of the 91st Bomb Group, US Army Air Force, with Sergeant William D 'Bill' Pulliam a photographic officer, at RAF Bassingbourn, Cambridgeshire, c.1944.

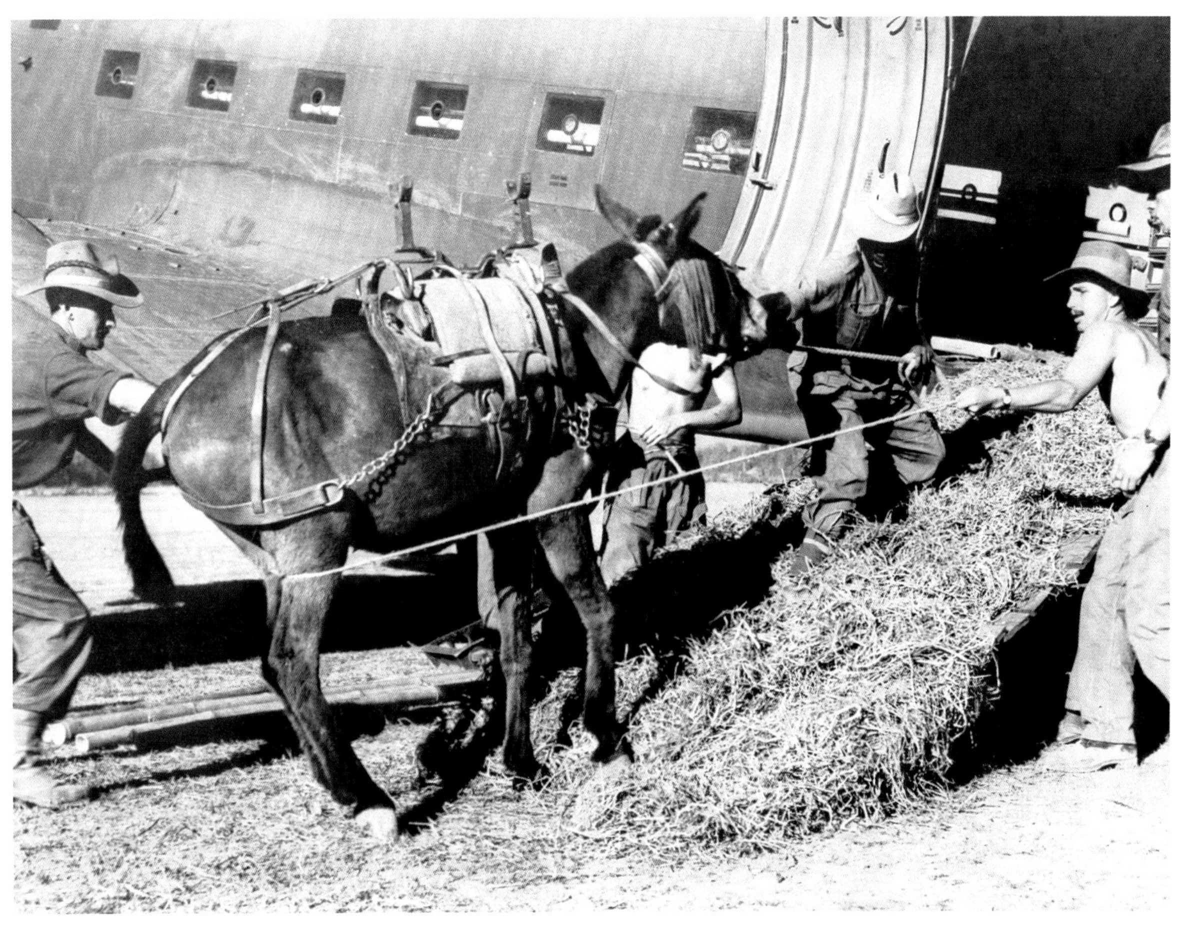

A reluctant mule is coaxed into a C-47 transport aircraft in India, 1944. Mules were used extensively to carry supplies for troops in the jungles of India and Burma, including these Chindits preparing to fight behind enemy lines.

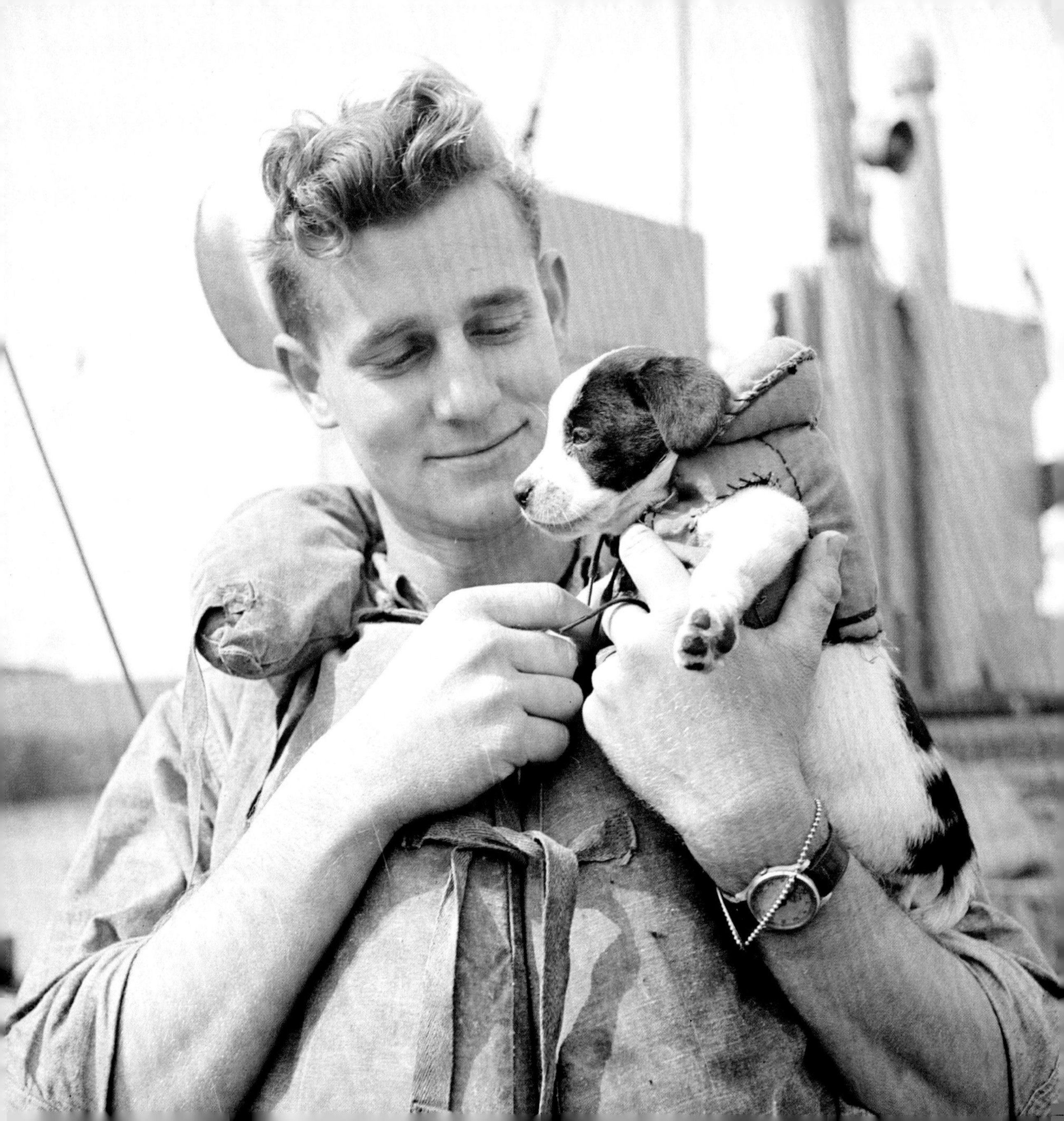

Swabby the puppy accompanies his owner, Chief Machinist's Mate Edward Hutton, US Navy, in an invasion craft for the Allied landings in Normandy, France, on 6 June 1944. Swabby is wearing a life preserver especially made by the crew of Eddie's ship.

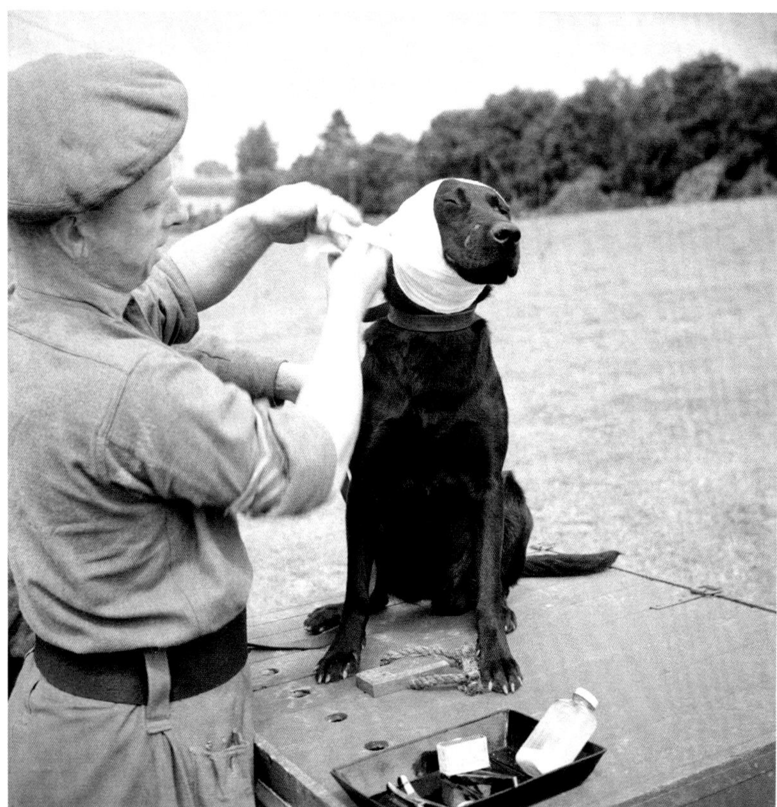

During the Second World War dangerous new roles were given to dogs.
A sergeant of the Royal Army Veterinary Corps bandages the wounded ear of Jasper, a mine-detecting dog, Bayeux, France, 5 July 1944.

An elderly man inspects the front paw of his dog, injured following a devastating V1 attack in Upper Norwood, London, July 1944. The man's wife was killed when their house was destroyed. The dog was hiding in the Morrison shelter, which saved him.

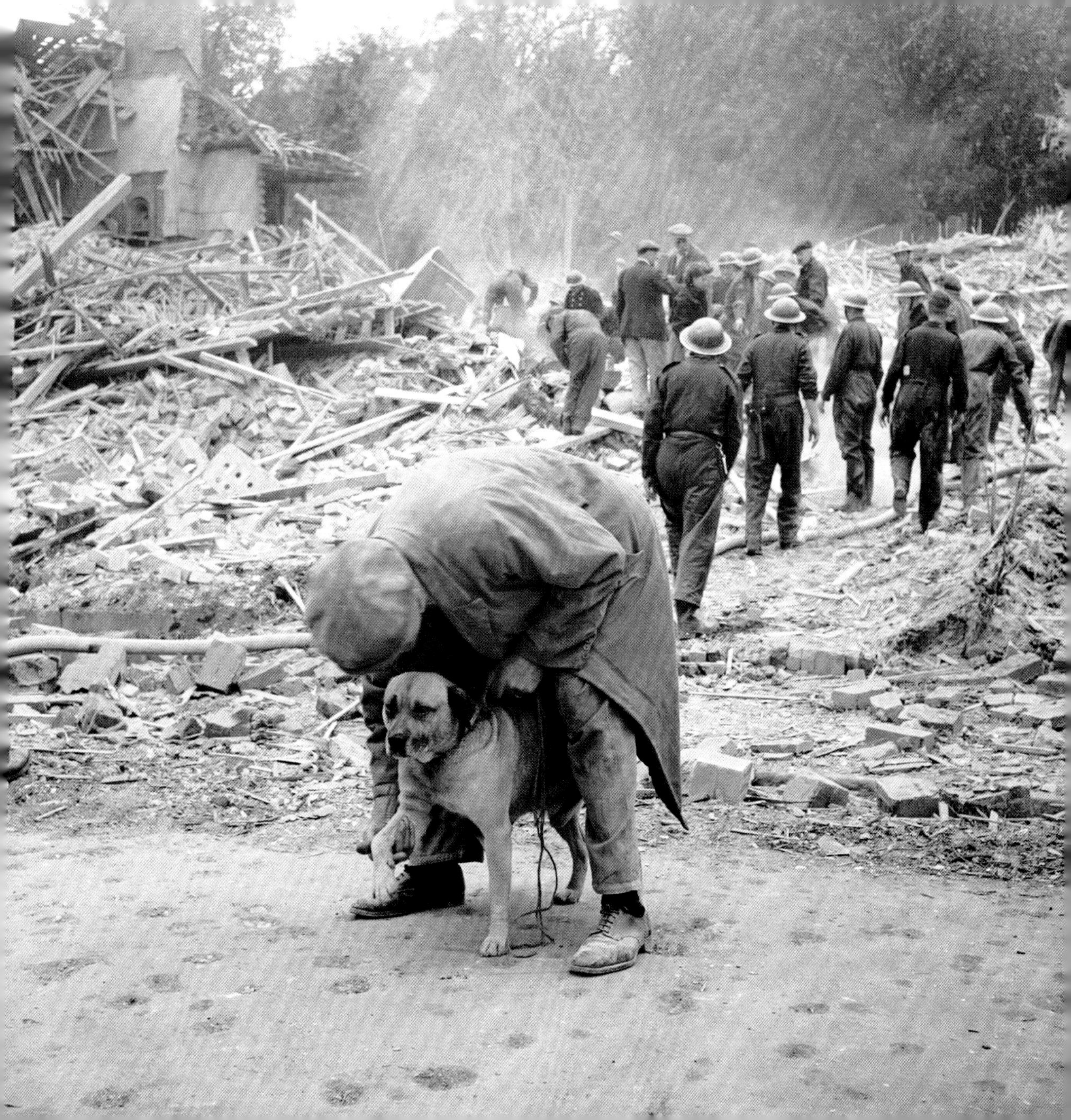

An ox, assisted by US marines, pulls a heavy load through thick mud in the Pacific theatre on Saipan in the Northern Mariana Islands, July 1944. Oxen were good military draught animals although slow and requiring large quantities of food.

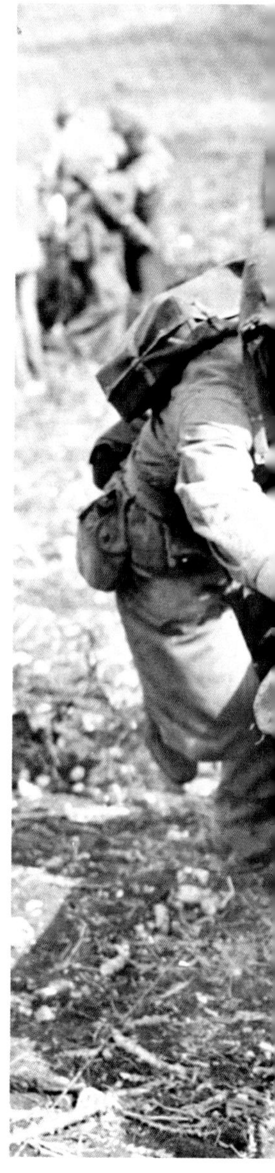

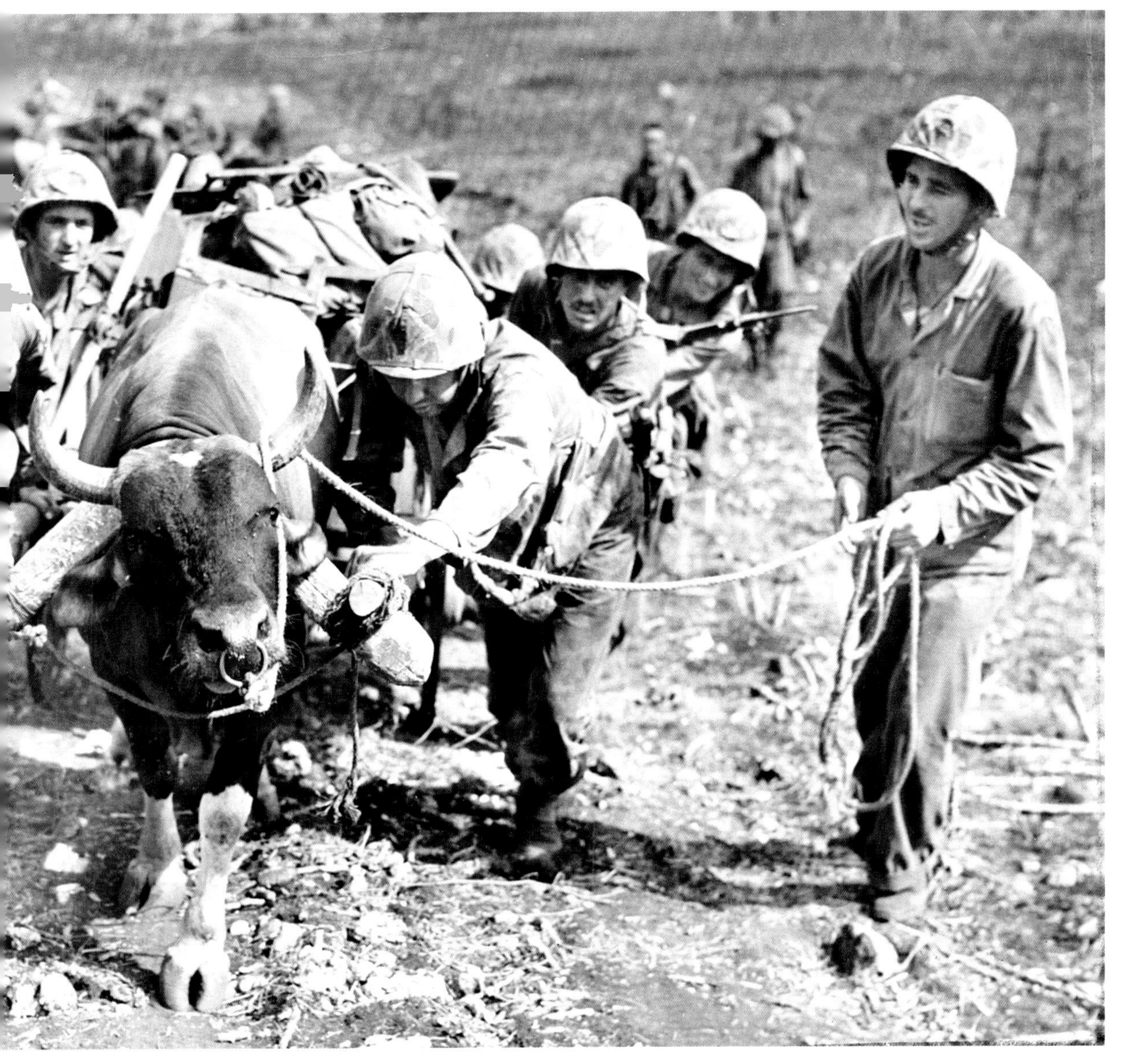

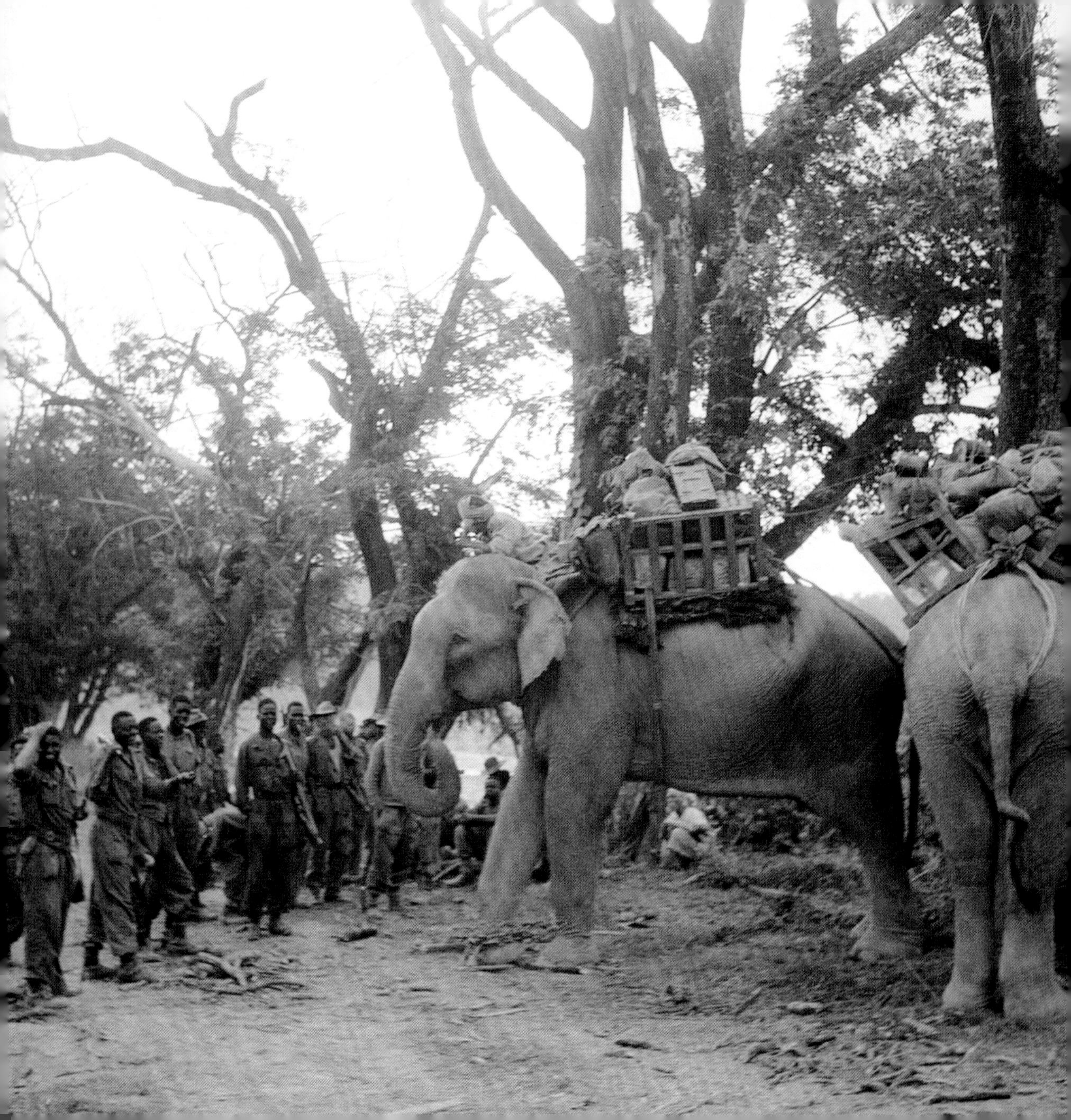

Troops of the 11th East African Division cheering elephants entering their base with supplies in the captured port of Kalewa on the Chindwin River, Burma, 5 January 1945. The elephants were captured from the Japanese during the advance towards the river.

Stafford of No. 5 Section, 'B' Dog Provost Company, Corps of Military Police, being trained by Corporal A Moffat, to jump over a high fence in a training centre in Klagenfurt, Austria, around June 1945.

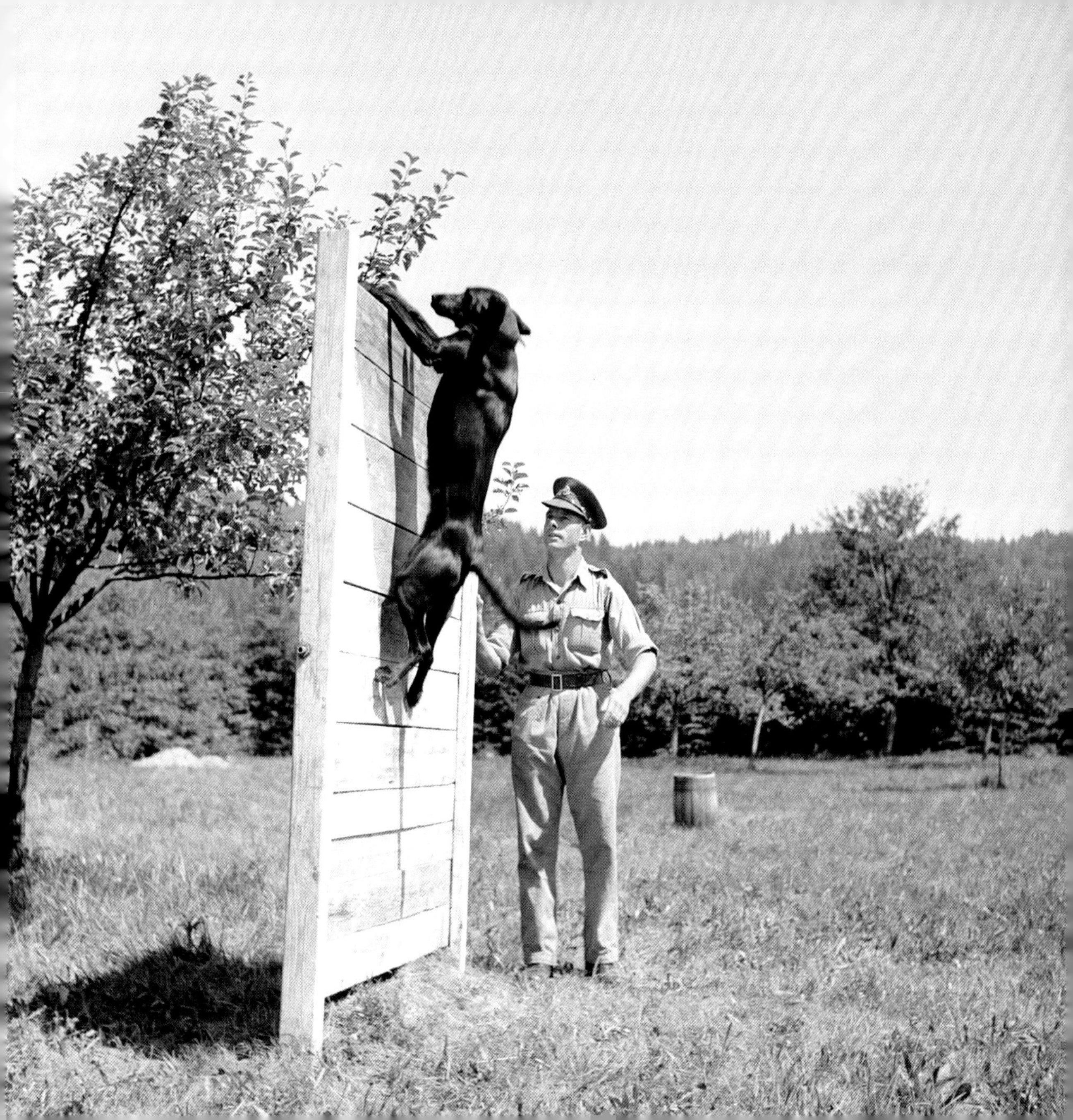

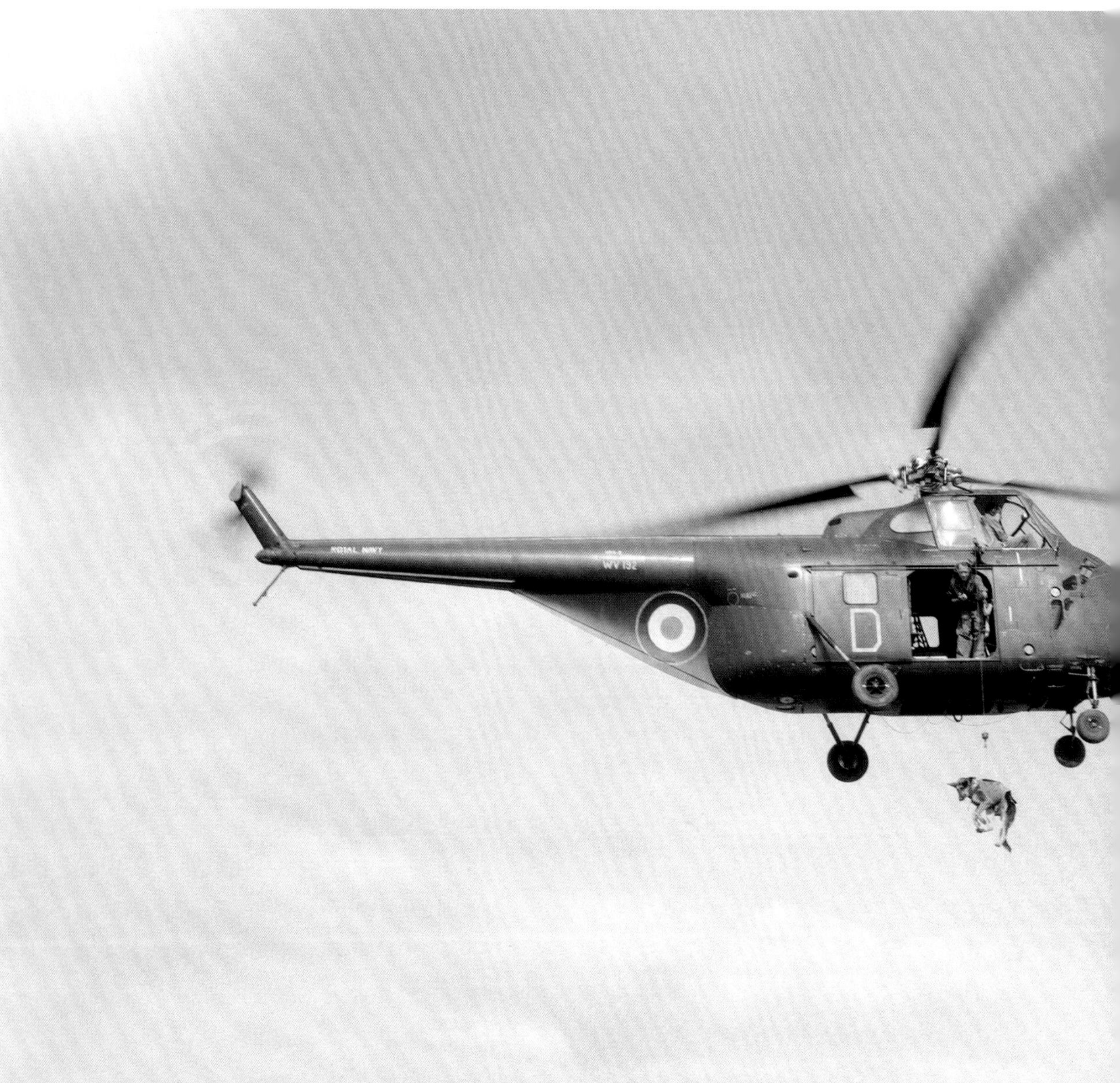
WV192
D

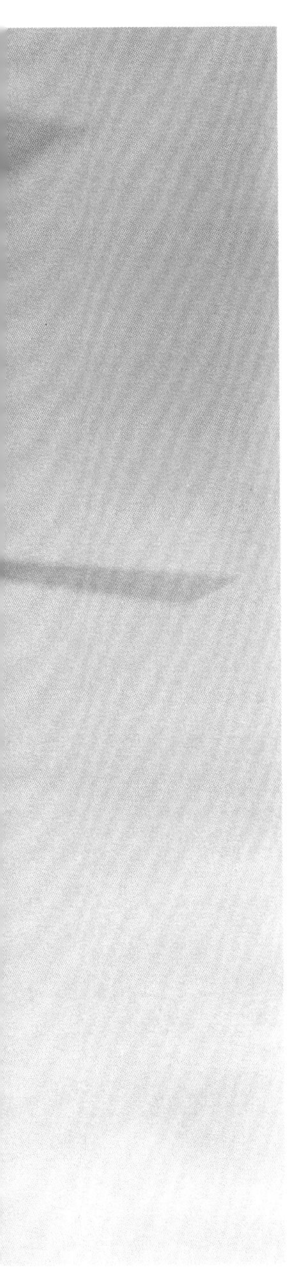

A tracker dog being hauled into a helicopter of No. 848 Squadron RAF after completing a task searching for insurgents in the jungles of Malaya in 1953.

The kitten mascot of the aircraft carrier HMS *Eagle* in the hammock made for her by the ship's sailmaker, 1956.

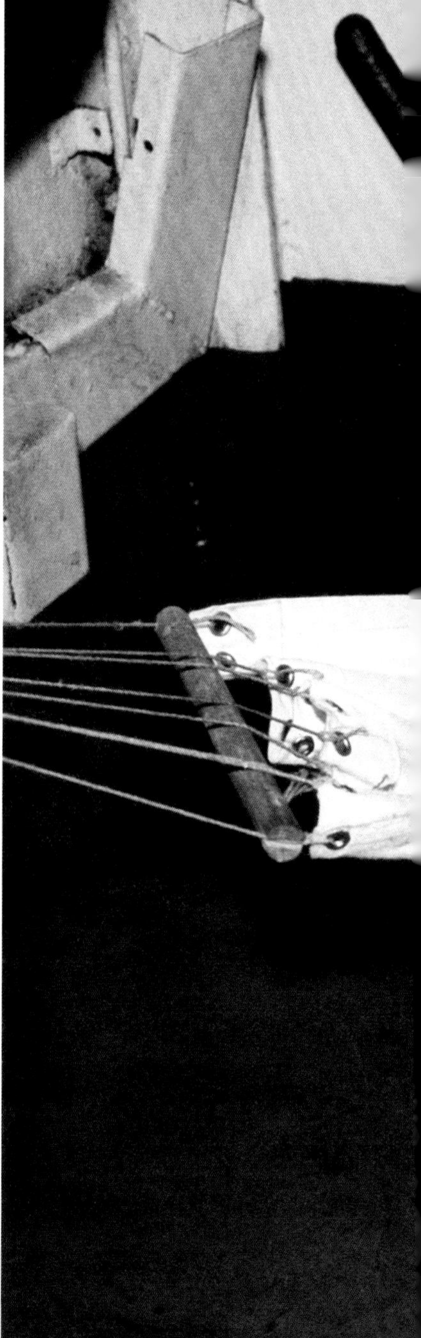

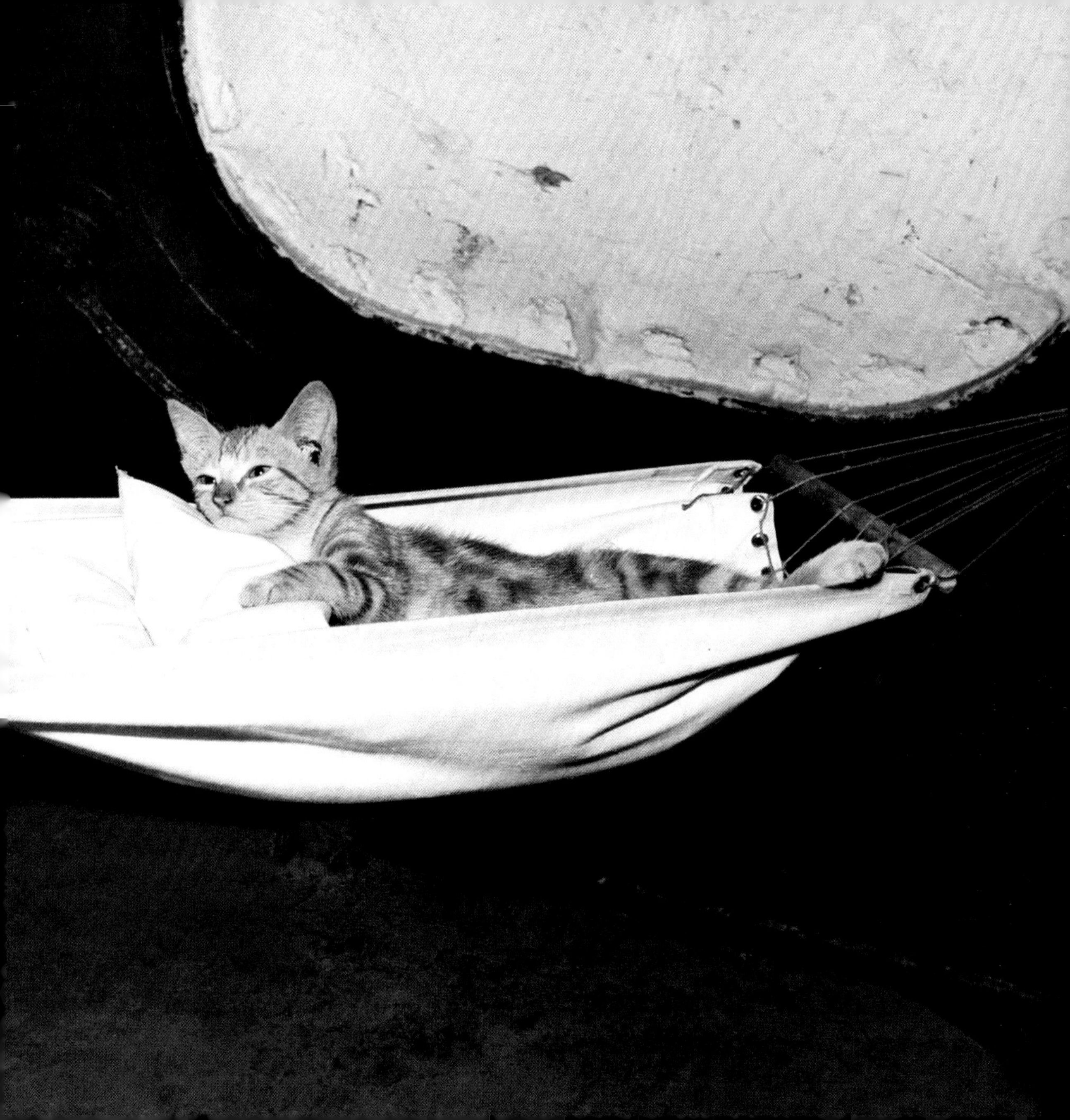

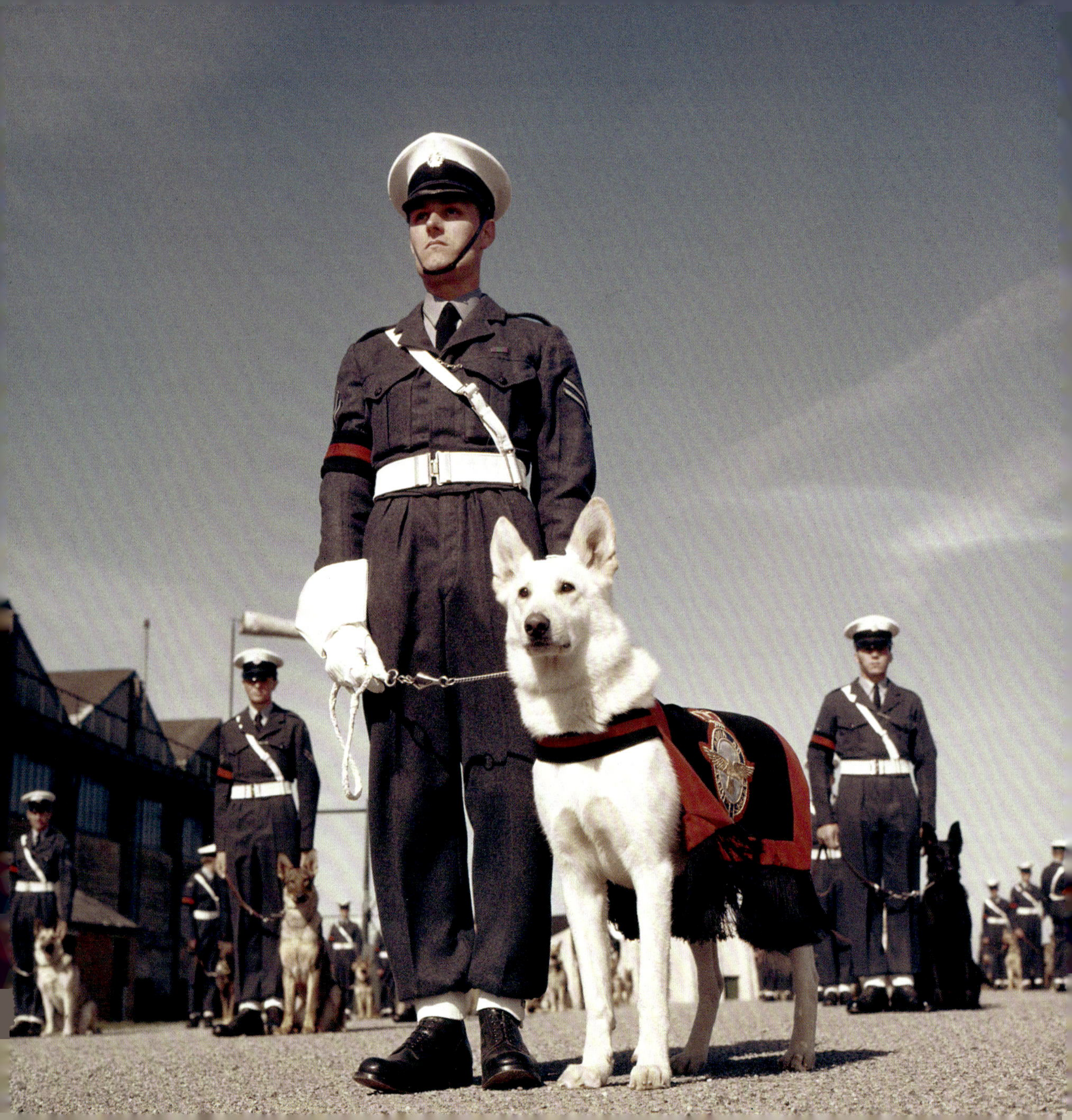

The RAF Police Dog Demonstration Team of 1958 at the RAF Police Depot at Netheravon, Wiltshire. In the foreground is 4686 Air Dog Comet, the team's mascot for their tenth anniversary Royal Tournament appearance, with Police Dog Handler Corporal J Tait.

An RAF Air Dog and his handler guard an Avro Blue Steel nuclear bomb from its storage to the awaiting Avro Vulcan B.2A, at RAF Scampton, Lincolnshire, home of No. 617 Squadron, February 1963.

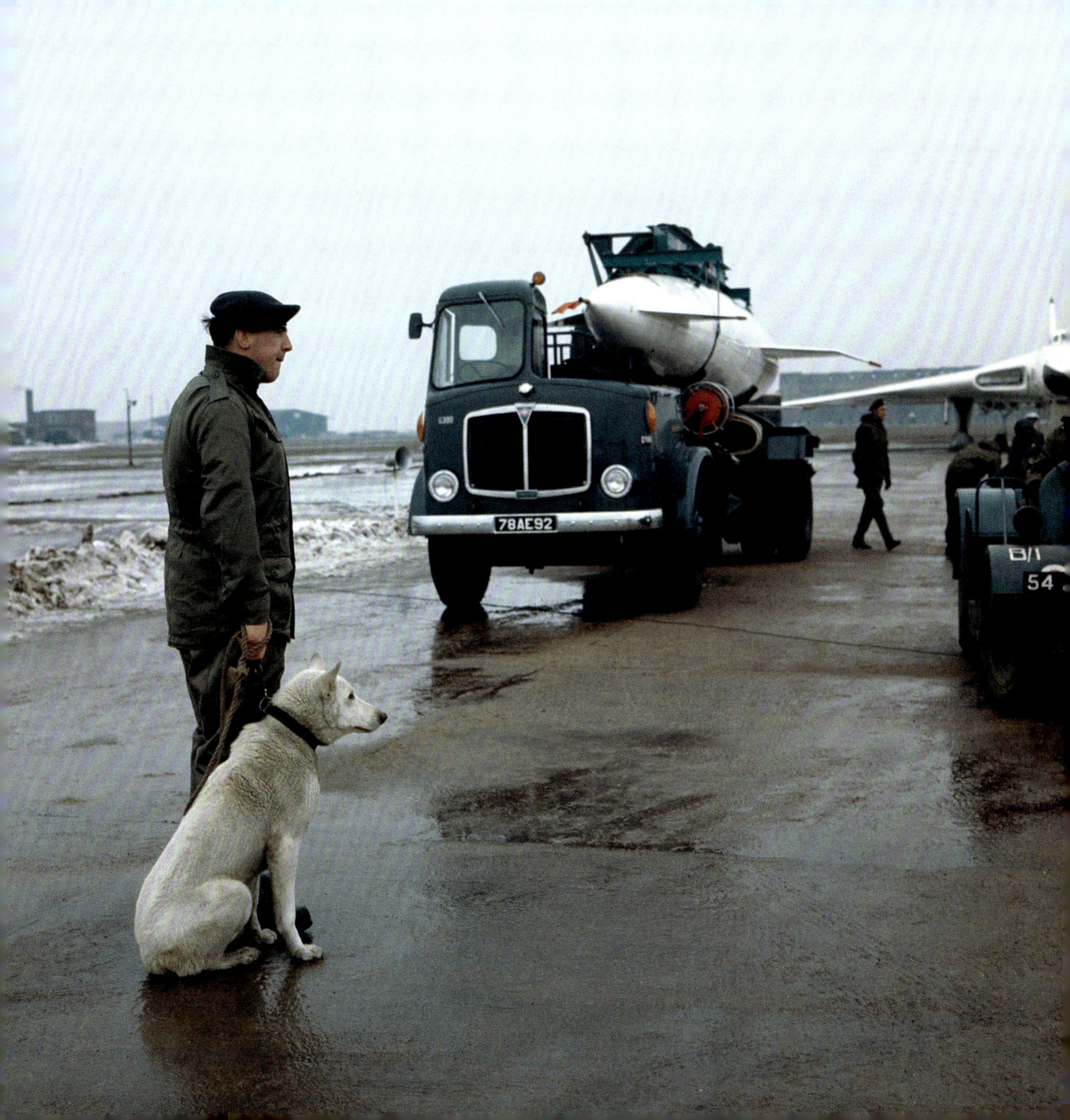
78AE92
B/1
54

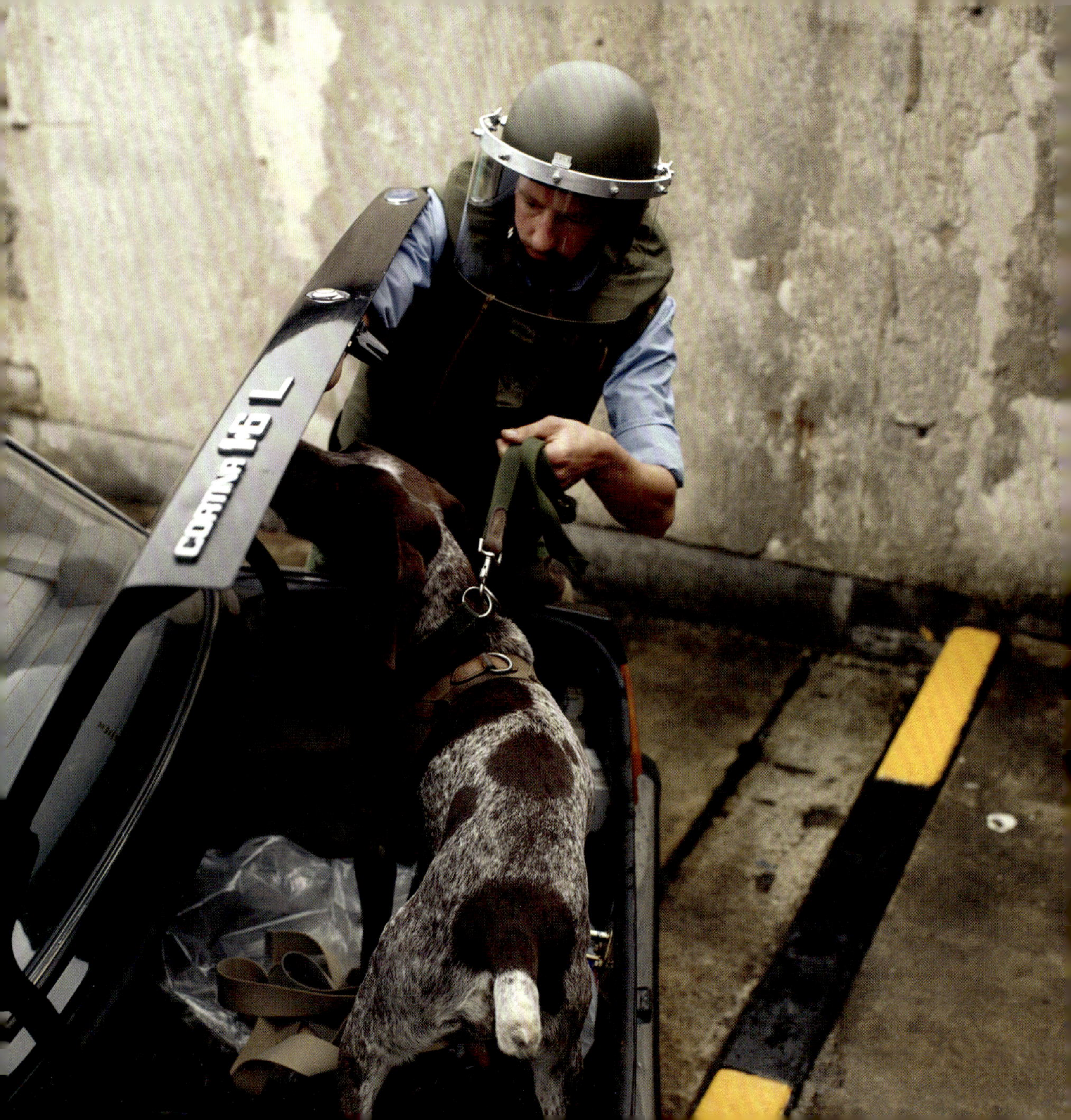
CORTINA 16 L

A German Shorthaired Pointer, while working as an RAF police sniffer dog, searches a car boot for weapons and explosives following an attack by Provisional IRA on RAF personnel based at RAF Laarbruch, Germany in 1988.

A search dog wearing eye and foot protection before travelling in a Boeing Chinook in Nahr-e Saraj District, Helmand Province, Afghanistan, October 2011. The boots protect against the hot stones and help avoid contaminating evidence at IED sites.

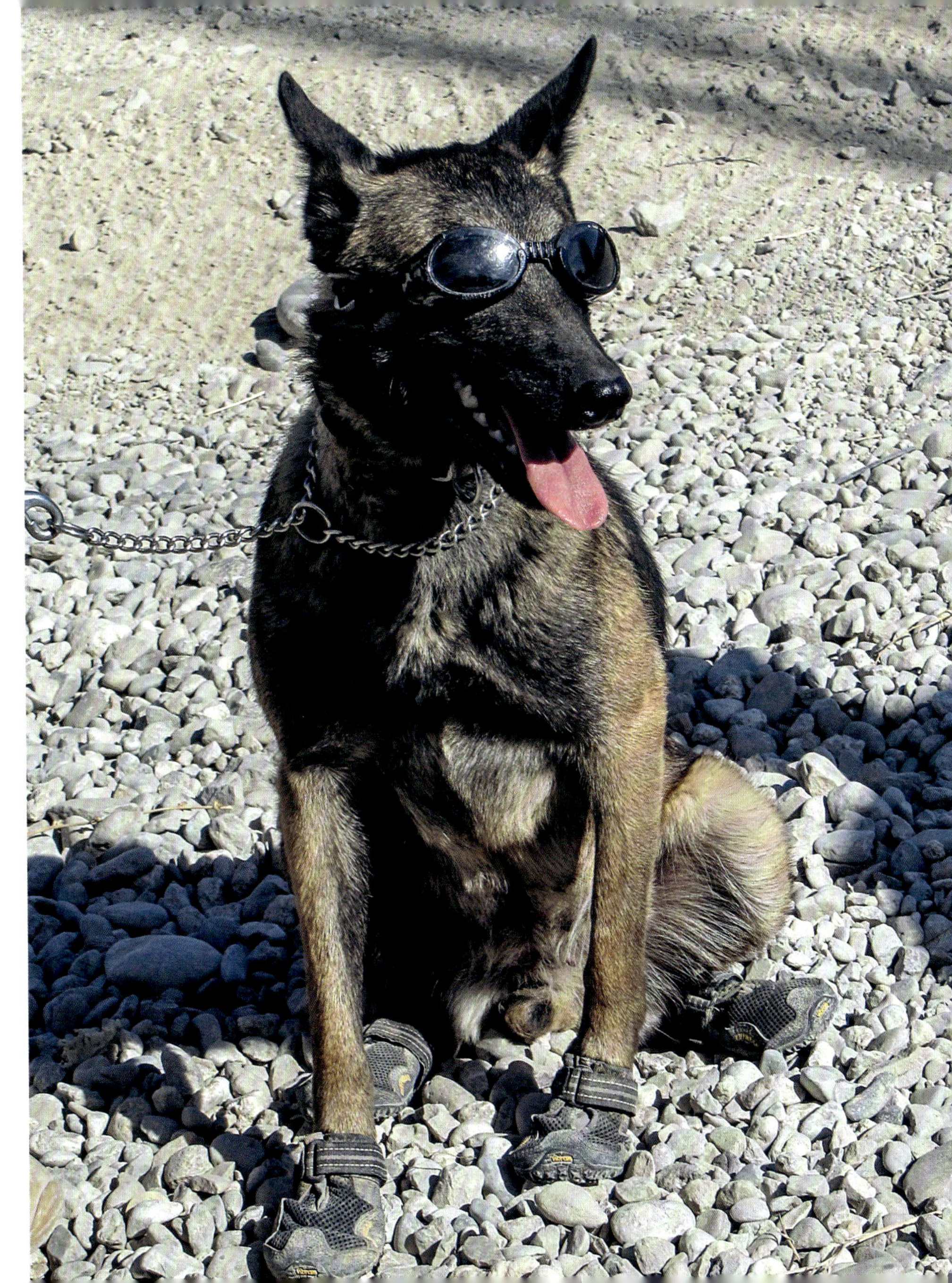

Devil the dog, with female handler, part of the Explosive Ordnance Disposal (EOD) and Search Task Force, conducting compound searches, Nahr-e Saraj District, Helmand Province, Afghanistan, January 2012.

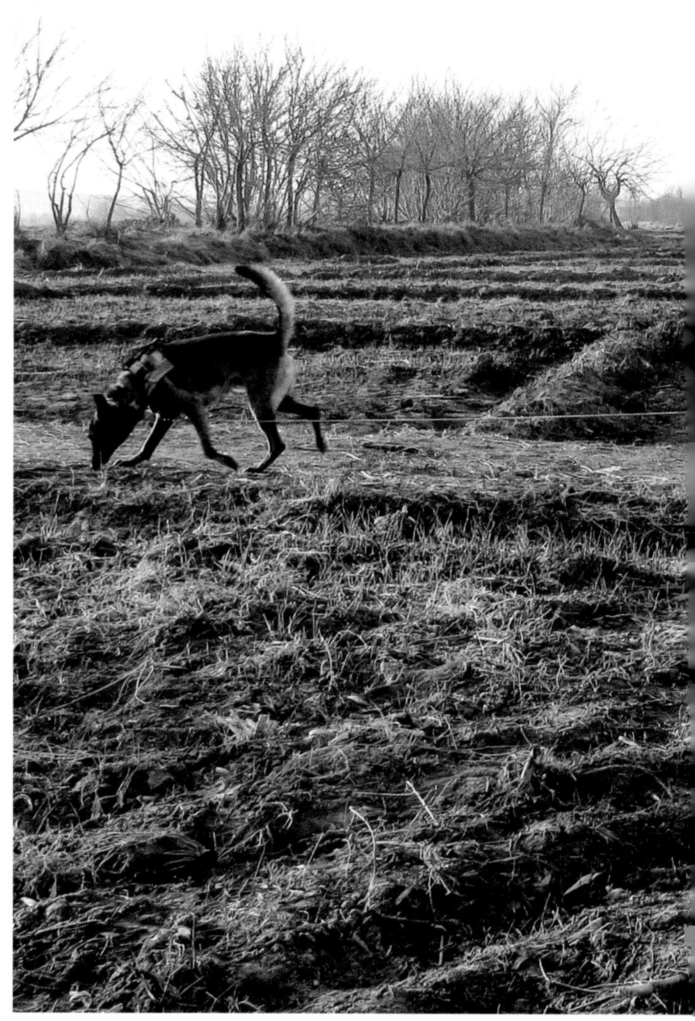

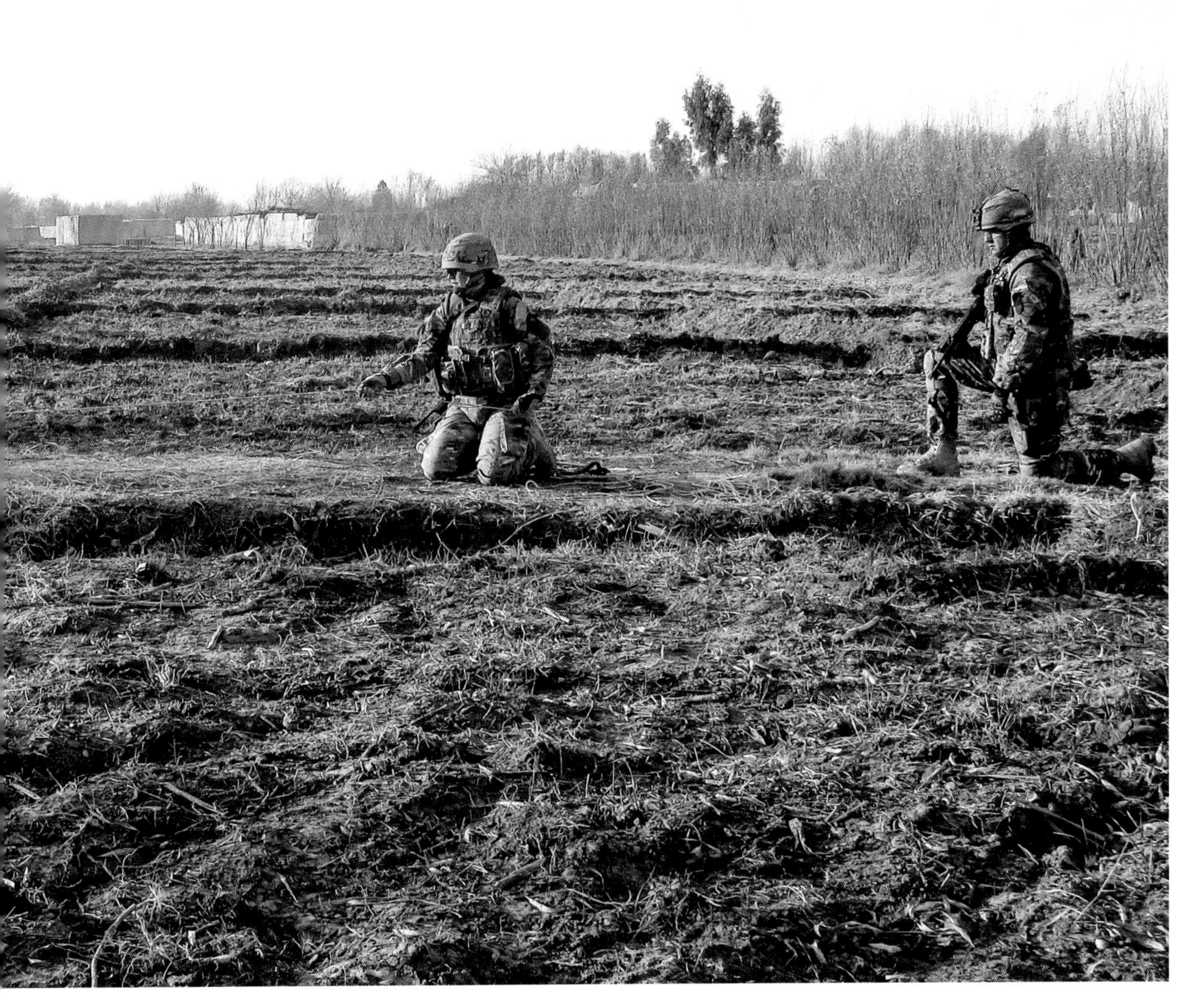

Image List

A 175 (detail), Q 31798 (detail), Q 54993, Q 1424, Q 15603, CO 1414, Q 2213, Q 54973, Q 54124, Q 5941, Q 50670, Q 6475, Q 8463, Q 30918, Q 10957, Q 9247, Q 105525 © the rights holder, Q 16175, HU 36167, D 984, A 175, A 3998, D 442, F 2672, D 1639, HU 128847, HU 63823, E 3593, H 12985, D 5937, COL 156 © N Huntingford, HU 45623, CH 8999, FRE 9719, EA 30, CH 11978, FRE 5671, EA 20831, OWIL 25488, B 6496, D 21224, NYF 31412, SE 2823, NA 25683, A 32632, A 33564, RAF-T 589, RAF-T 3615, CT 446, DC 5362 © Taylor, DC 5380 © Taylor.

About the Author

Simon Offord is an archivist and currently a curator in the Second World War and Mid-20th Century Conflict Team at IWM. He has worked at IWM since 2001, working firstly in the Department of Documents, with curatorial responsibility for the letters, diaries, memoirs and other paper-based records relating to the Second World War in IWM's archives. In 2020 he was the Lead Curator for the *Refugees: Forced to Flee* exhibition at IWM London.

Acknowledgements

The author would like to thank the following IWM colleagues for their support: John Delaney and Chris Cooper (Joint Heads of the Second World War and Mid-20th Century Conflict team), Madeleine James (Publishing & Brand Licensing Manager), Lara Bateman (Publishing Officer), Helen Mavin (Head of Photographs), Anthony Richards (Head of Documents and Sound), as well as the many other colleagues involved in publishing this book. My gratitude also to Juliet Gardiner, author of *The Animals' War: Animals in Wartime from the First World War to the Present Day* for the very useful information. Thank you to my parents and family for all their support over the years, and to my darling wife Sabrina for everything.